D0458553

POWER, TERROR, PEACE, AND WAR

POWER,
TERROR,
PEACE,
AND WAR

*America's Grand Strategy
in a World at Risk*

WALTER RUSSELL MEAD

A COUNCIL ON FOREIGN RELATIONS BOOK

Alfred A. Knopf  *New York* 2004

A portion of this work previously appeared in Foreign Affairs.

Founded in 1921, the Council on Foreign on Foreign Relations is an independent, national membership organization and a nonpartisan center for scholars dedicated to producing and disseminating ideas so that individual and corporate members, as well as policymakers, journalists, students, and interested citizens in the United States and other countries, can better understand the world and the foreign policy choices facing the United States and other governments. The Council does this by convening meetings; conducting a wide-ranging Studies program; publishing Foreign Affairs, *the preeminent journal covering international affairs and U.S. foreign policy; maintaining a diverse membership; sponsoring Independent Task Forces; and providing up-to-date information about the world and U.S. foreign policy on the Council's website, www.cfr.org.*

THE COUNCIL TAKES NO INSTITUTIONAL POSITION ON POLICY ISSUES AND HAS NO AFFILIATION WITH THE U.S. GOVERNMENT. ALL STATEMENTS OF FACT AND EXPRESSIONS OF OPINION CONTAINED IN ALL ITS PUBLICATIONS ARE THE SOLE RESPONSIBILITY OF THE AUTHOR OR AUTHORS.

Library of Congress Cataloging-in-Publication Data
Mead, Walter Russell.
Power, terror, peace, and war : America's grand strategy in a world at risk / Walter Russell Mead—1st ed.
p. cm.
"A Council on Foreign Relations book."
Includes bibliographical references and index.
ISBN *1-4000-4237-2 (alk. paper)*
1. United States—Foreign relations—21st century.
2. War on Terrorism, 2001– I. Title.
JZ1480 .M43 2004
327.73—dc22   2003067277

Manufactured in the United States of America
First Edition

To Allen Adler

The glory of friendship is not the outstretched hand,
nor the kindly smile, nor the joy of companionship;
it's the spiritual inspiration that comes to one
when he discovers that someone else believes in him
and is willing to trust him with his friendship.
—Ralph Waldo Emerson

CONTENTS

POWER, TERROR, PEACE, AND WAR

The American Crisis

L ate in the summer of 2001, I saw the movie *Pearl Harbor*. Odd duck that I am, it was neither the forgettable love story nor the spectacular special effects that made the deepest impression on me. Rather, I thought about how hideous it must have felt to watch the Pandora's box of war open and know that the future had suddenly taken a terrible turn. I also thought about how American foreign policy makers must have felt on that day as the news of the attacks poured in and they realized that their failures and negligence had helped expose their country and their fellow citizens to a monstrous danger.

Less than a month later, I knew much more what that day must have felt like. As smoke and debris swirled through the streets of my own city of New York, and as I watched my fellow citizens, soot-stained, grimy, and inexpressibly weary trudging north from Lower Manhattan like so many refugees, my sorrow, anger, and shock were matched by feelings of shame and regret. Once again, Americans had been surprised by an attack from overseas; once again, we had failed to prevent the beginning of a terrible new chapter in the history of war.

The twelve years between the fall of the Berlin Wall in 1989 and the attacks of September 2001 were lost years in American foreign policy. From November 9, 1989, when the Berlin Wall came down, through September 11, 2001, three administrations from two parties beguiled themselves with pleasing illusions about the health of the American system even as formidable challenges to that system were assembling offshore. It was a bipartisan age of narcissism and hubris. Ignoring the complexities of Francis Fukuyama's groundbreaking book, a current of opinion blissfully concluded that history was over and the United States had won. Rogue states might sometimes vex us, it was felt, but no fundamental security challenges would arise, and our allies were with us. How could they not be? The United States was the strongest military power in the world and the standard-bearer of the democratic and capitalist ideologies that had triumphed so completely over their communist rivals.

Conservatives tended to use terms like Charles Krauthammer's "unipolar world" to describe the new age of world politics; Secretary of State Madeleine Albright preferred to call the United States the "indispensable nation." Both terms meant that the United States was in charge of the international system, and faced no serious and powerful challengers to it.

There were, of course, dangers. Democrats worried that Republican unilateralism would lose international goodwill through resistance to such initiatives as the Kyoto Protocol and the International Criminal Court and that the United States could squander its once-in-a-millennium opportunity to build a global system based on law. Republicans worried that Democratic fecklessness on defense would open the door to a future challenge to American supremacy from China and that in the meantime the failure to build a missile defense system could quickly give nuclear-armed rogue states a window of opportunity in which they could blackmail the United States.

In both cases the concern was that foolish actions now could endanger the American project sometime in the future. There was little sense in the foreign policy establishment that the American system and indeed the United States faced urgent dangers in the much shorter term.

While Samuel Huntington warned about a potential "clash of civilizations" and many others focused on China as an emerging potential threat, for most American policy makers during those lost years, the United States was the only real actor in the international system. If we did the right things, good consequences would follow and our intentions would prevail. The international system was not just unipolar; it was monothelete—there was only one effective will operating in the world, the will of the United States. Our power was so great that once we knew our own minds and gave the lead, others would follow. Most would follow willingly, entranced by the beauties of our soft power. Some would come reluctantly, but our other forms of power were compelling enough to ensure compliance when soft power failed.

The real situation in the world, it has become increasingly plain since September 11, was quite different. During those lost years a climate of opinion on the radical fringes of the Muslim world had coalesced into a mass movement, and acquired the ambition and the ability to make war on the United States and the American system. With a handful of exceptions, our strongest Cold War alliances were fraying and disintegrating. In the aftermath of the September attacks some of our oldest and closest allies would not just deplore American leadership, they would actively oppose it. Beyond the circle of allies, the international political climate also turned rapidly and radically against the United States. Poll after poll showed that the United States was increasingly seen as the chief threat to world peace. Within months of September 11, the indispensable nation was becoming the indefensible nation.

What was happening was not simply that an abrasive Bush administration was needlessly antagonizing otherwise loyal and friendly allies. That was certainly part of the story, but beyond this the aftermath of September 11 was demonstrating in no uncertain terms that the American project was no longer as popular in the world as it had once been. France, meanwhile, intoxicated with its greatest prominence in international affairs since it surrendered to Hitler, rallied a worldwide coalition of peoples and regimes to its side against the United States with an enthusiasm that could be neither denied nor accounted for simply by disagreements over Iraq.

This book appears at a time when the United States is bitterly divided over what those attacks meant and how we should best respond. The months since September 11, 2001, have been unremitting months of international crisis as the United States has quarreled with some countries, invaded others, and found itself bogged down in difficult guerrilla campaigns in far-flung corners of the world. The deepest and most bitter battles over foreign policy since the Vietnam era are convulsing the country, and our leaders tell us that we remain vulnerable to mass terror and that our enemies, though weakened, still have the will and the power to launch devastating attacks.

Since the attacks I have visited more than a dozen countries around the world and talked with diplomats, journalists, students, national leaders, and regular citizens. Sometimes I came as a State Department–sponsored visitor, not representing the U.S. government or speaking an official line, but trying to help foreigners understand the changes in American society and foreign policy—and trying myself to understand the foreign responses to us. At other times I have traveled privately—on book tours, study tours, and vacations. I have talked to some of America's enemies, and I have talked to many of our friends. I have heard and felt the deep and often agonizing mix of sympathy, anger, incredulity, and hostility that so many intelligent and thoughtful people around the world feel as they contemplate the Bush administration's response to September 11. I have also visited more than a dozen American states, speaking to audiences large and small, appearing on radio call-in shows, attending conferences with scholars and experts, visiting high schools and colleges, and doing my best to listen to what Americans think about the state of the world and the state of this embattled nation.

What follows is my best effort at describing what America is trying to do in the world, why things have gone so terribly wrong, what the Bush administration tried to do, where it has and where it has not been successful, and what we need to do to get American foreign policy back on track. I start with the idea that there is an American project—a grand strategic vision of what it is that the United States seeks to build in the world. This project—to protect our own domestic security while building a peaceful world order of democratic states linked by common values and sharing a common prosperity—has deep roots in the American past. In *Special Providence* I tried to show how the various elements of this project can be traced all the way back through American history, and how continuing national debates over how best to define and achieve this project (or whether to try it at all) have shaped both American and world history over the last two centuries. The bitter debates over foreign policy since the attacks of September 11 are the latest stage in a long national conversation over the best way to proceed with the American project under changing circumstances. Even as the debates rage, however, most Americans continue to support the idea that the United States should be leading the effort to build a safer, peaceful, prosperous, and democratic world.

I can't claim that anything in this book will provide America's final answer to the difficult new questions that history is asking us. But I hope that my attempts to ask the right questions and sketch out the best answers I can come up with will encourage and assist others as American society moves to cope with the latest in a long line of challenges to our national project.

"Never apologize, never explain" may be a good motto for heroes in Western adventure sagas, but it doesn't work as well for writers, and especially for writers on American foreign policy. A book like this one needs generous helpings both of apology and of explanation. American foreign policy may be the most complex subject in the world. Economics, political science, history and the philosophy of history, culture, religion, the nature of human nature: American foreign policy touches on them all. And while American foreign policy is studied in great detail by professionals and scholars, it must ultimately be debated and decided by tens of millions of voters who have neither the time nor perhaps the inclination to immerse themselves in briefing papers, task force reports, and long scholarly texts.

If in trying to bridge the gap between professionals and the educated lay public this book sometimes falls into the river rather than gracefully spanning it, I hope readers on both banks will do their best to supplement the weakness of my performance by the generosity of their imagination.

Actually, the chasm this book tries to bridge doesn't just divide "knowledgeable experts" from "ignorant laypeople." Most of us alternate between those roles. The technically proficient economist may and often does know less about diplomatic history than the educated lay reader; the international lawyer knows next to nothing about military tactics. The expert on Chinese history is completely at sea when the subject turns to Brazil.

We live in a world of specialists, but American foreign policy demands generalists. American national strategy tries to integrate economics, politics, military studies, and many other subjects to create and support an international system. It seems to me that only a generalist can write a book about American foreign policy as a large, single system; it also seems pretty clear that such a book will be flawed. Generalists are superficially mistaken about a great many subjects; specialists are profoundly mistaken about a few.

Whether this is more of an explanation or an apology I leave to the reader, but there is one more thing I ought to say to introduce this book and prepare the reader for what is coming.

I have not started this book at the true ground zero of American foreign policy: I have not attempted to provide a comprehensive moral defense of the American project in the world. On the whole, I think that the aims and methods of American foreign policy, while sometimes mistaken and often questionable, are reasonably consistent with the happiness and advancement of humanity as a whole. I am less sure of this than I am of another truth: that the destruction of the American system in the world would lead to far more misery and danger than we now see, and that the fall of American power would be a catastrophe not only for Americans but for millions and billions who live beyond our frontiers, including many of those who hate us and would destroy us if they could.

For these reasons, I have written this book as an advocate of the American project, and the purpose of my intervention is not to persuade Americans that we should or could do something different and better in the world, but to show them better ways of achieving goals which, from where I stand, seem to be about as moral and as practical as could be expected.

I realize that there are other points of view. American foreign policy is even more controversial than usual these days. Not only is there a sharp debate within the United States, but the international discussion of the rights and wrongs of American foreign policy is more intense than it has been for many a year. I plan to participate in that discussion, but not here. This book is already too full.

The book you are about to read has four parts. Part

One, "The American Project," looks at what American foreign policy has been about, what our national grand strategy has been. "The Gathering Storm," Part Two, looks at the forces that in the last twenty years have been undermining American power and setting the stage for a new era of confrontation and danger even as many Americans were congratulating themselves on having reached the end of history. Part Three, "Revival in Action," is a look at the forces shaping the Bush administration's foreign policy and analyzes both the strengths and the limits of the administration's approach to world politics and the war on terror. The last section, "The Future of American Foreign Policy," describes the issues and the approaches that in my view should shape our foreign policy in the near future.

PART ONE

The American Project

ONE

No Angel in Our Whirlwind

The concept of grand strategy comes to us from the German military writer Carl von Clausewitz. Tactics, said Clausewitz, was about winning battles; strategy was about winning campaigns and wars. Grand strategy was about deciding what wars to fight. Tactics was for generals and other officers; strategy was the business of the general military headquarters; and grand strategy was for ministers and kings.

Not anymore. Clausewitz's vision of leadership and strategy dates from the image Joseph Addison developed to describe military leadership in his 1705 poem "The Campaign," on the Duke of Marlborough's victory at the Battle of Blenheim. Addison depicts an organizational, professional heroism that reflected the new realities of the modern world. Leaders no longer showed their courage as Homeric heroes had done in personal combat, but in their cool-headed ability to shape gigantic events. As the Battle of Blenheim raged, Addison wrote that Marlborough:

> Amidst confusion, horror, and despair,
> Examin'd all the dreadful scenes of war:
> In peaceful thought the field of death survey'd,

> *To fainting squadrons sent the timely aid,*
> *Inspir'd repuls'd battalions to engage,*
> *And taught the dreadful battle where to rage.*
> *So when an angel by divine command*
> *With rising tempests shaks a guilty land,*
> *Such as of late o'er pale Britannia past,*
> *Calm and serene he drives the furious blast;*
> *And, pleas'd th' Almighty's orders to perform,*
> *Rides in the whirlwind, and directs the storm.* *

That may have been the way things worked at Blenheim and on the Prussian general staff, but it is not the way things work in America today. There is no angel in our whirlwind, no central guiding intelligence organizing American foreign policy into a coherent whole. Our civil society is larger, more dynamic, and more global in its reach than anything Clausewitz saw in Germany, and our officials are weaker than the elite that governed Germany in Bismarck and Clausewitz's day. Clausewitzian grand strategy requires long-term thinking; American officials are condemned by the realities of domestic politics to short-term thinking tied to election cycles and, for presidents, the two-term limit. Conventional Clausewitzian grand strategy also requires central direction. A Bismarck could ignore the German Reichstag and, with his thirty-eight years in power in first Prussia and then the German Empire, subordinate the bureaucracy to his will. No American president, much less secretary of state, ever gets this kind of power. Then there is Congress, a collection of whirlwinds in which angels are notably scarce, consisting of two houses each with its own set of rules, procedures, and powerful committees, and each jealous of its own powers and eager to check presidents and impose the (sometimes conflicting) visions of its power-

---

* Joseph Addison, "The Campaign," in *The Works of the English Poets, with Prefaces, Biographical and Critical,* ed. Samuel Johnson (London: H. Baldwin, 1779), 23:51–67.

ful members and constituencies on American foreign policy.

The ever-shifting views of public opinion set and reset the boundaries of the possible for officeholders. When an American president is doing well in the polls, he can defy Congress and impose his will on the process; when the poll numbers fall, so does his power in Washington. As a result, American foreign policy reflects the vector of the impulses and interests, convictions and half-conscious biases of large numbers of people. It is a mall, not a boutique—a conglomeration of sometimes competing retailers offering a wide variety of products to a miscellaneous assemblage of consumers from every race and class rather than a single store with a focused strategy targeting a handful of carefully selected items for a narrow market. Nobody wants everything in the mall, and everybody thinks some of the merchandise on display is just awful, but most people can find something they like.

The foreign policy of the American government, however, is only one part of a much broader and more influential enterprise: the foreign policy of the American people. Billions of butterflies flap their wings to shape this mighty storm. There is the business world, including everything from corner grocery stores to giant corporations active across the entire surface of the globe with annual revenues larger than that of many member states of the United Nations. Those are the various types of media ranging from television networks to the blogosphere, and there are all the commentators, editors, owners, and reporters in the media, each pursuing a vision of how to see and shape American foreign policy. There are labor unions, ethnic organizations, chambers of commerce, churches, synagogues, human rights lobby groups, environmental organizations, antisweatshop organizers, foundations, humanitarian relief organizations, and dozens of other types of associations, often with conflicting agendas. They all seek to influence the foreign policy of the American government on various issues with various degrees of intensity and commitment; they also often carry out foreign policies of their own. Often, these private foreign policies are undertaken to counteract official policies of the U.S. government. Whatever the government is doing, Croatian Americans are supporting Croatia's efforts to flourish as an independent nation. Governors of American farm states drop in on Fidel Castro with the hope of opening new markets for their state's agricultural produce and of widening the loopholes in the U.S. embargo against the communist island. American corporations are seeking to change the trade policies of foreign countries. The American labor movement has an extensive network of relationships with labor movements in other countries. George Soros created the Open Society Institute in part to change the way central and eastern European countries were governed as they made the transition from communism. American environmentalist groups, sometimes in alliance with environmentalist groups in other countries, work to pressure foreign governments to control pesticides and pollutants, protect endangered species, and stop killing whales and cutting down tropical rain forests.

All of these efforts by policy makers, lobbyists, and citizens' groups are intentional attempts to change the world, but the most profound impact that the United States has on the rest of the world often comes from activities where we have no conscious intention to affect the rest of the world. We are minding our own business, we allow ourselves to think, hardly considering the consequences of our choices on others. The managers of an American pension fund, focusing on the financial well-being of their beneficiaries, can set off a crisis in some strategic country because they decide its bonds are no longer a safe investment. If American consumers decide that a synthetic fiber makes a more attractive halter top than natural fiber materials, there can be serious political and economic consequences abroad. If American capital markets become more efficient, allocating capital with greater effectiveness so that the average return on capital increases, then other countries will start to feel pressure to make similar changes in their own systems of capital allocation. If a powerful retailing technique, like franchising fried chicken and hamburger fast-food chains, catches on in the United States, then the chains will acquire the ambitions and the marketing know-how to change the eating habits and the merchandising patterns of other countries. The development of new computer software or a system like the Internet will change how the rest of the world does business. Opening the doors of higher education, the professions, and business to women in the United States creates all kinds of pressures in other societies, putting feminism on the agenda in other parts of the world, but also making the business environment tougher and more competitive because women are newly entitled to get into the game.

More profoundly, because the United States is such a powerful economic force in the world and because it is committed to let capitalism and free market enterprise develop relatively unhindered by government regulation, the United States helps set the economic agenda for most of the rest of the world. Foreign governments, companies, and consumers must live in a world capitalist system whose pace and intensity are largely (though not entirely or exclusively) set by innovations tried and decisions made in the United States.

Finally, American grand strategy has another quality that a Clausewitz would find disturbing: a messianic dimension. For many generations most Americans seem to have believed that American society was the best possible society and that the rest of the world would be better off if they became more like us. From very early in our history missionaries and others have gone off to help foreigners understand this better. But the national messiah complex reached a new high after the invention of nuclear weapons. Now that nuclear war, or the use of new and ever-proliferating types of weapons of mass destruction, threatens the continuation of human civilization, or even of human life, the American project of world order–building is increasingly seen as a matter of life and death for the whole human race. Those who hold this view believe we cannot allow the world to simply go on as it did in the past, with nations and civilizations dueling for supremacy heedless of the cost in human suffering. In the end it is not possible to understand either the American foreign policy debate or the passions it generates in a democratic society without understanding the great stakes for which so many of us think we play.

Partly because our overall role in the world is so complex and so little subject to the conscious control of any single person, when Americans think about foreign policy, we usually think about specific issues rather than the broad general shape of America's place in the world. We debate trade policy, the war in Iraq, the role of the UN Security Council, but we seldom step back to discuss the fundamental architecture of America's world policy as a whole. This is beginning to change. After September 11, and even more with the debate over the Second Gulf War, we have started to see a national debate over our engagement with the rest of the world. The controversy over the foreign policy of the Bush administration was caught up, as it should have been, in a much broader debate over what I am calling the American project: the overall impact of American society (including our government) on the rest of the world.

Just because we don't have a Bismarck directing our national destiny from decade to decade doesn't mean that our engagement with the world doesn't have a shape. We do not live in a Tolstoyan world where individual leaders and intentions have no weight. It matters who the president is. If Theodore Roosevelt and not Woodrow Wilson had been president when World War I broke out, American and world history might have taken a very different turn. Ideas also matter. Without neoconservativism, George W. Bush might be choosing among a different set of options. The point is not that individuals and individual ideas do not count, but rather that so many individuals and ideas matter in American foreign policy that what the nation is doing is generally larger and more complex than what any individual intends or, perhaps, understands.

More than this, over the long term, American foreign policy is not just random noise—280 million monkeys tapping furiously on 280 million keyboards. There may not be an angel in our whirlwind, but the whirlwind's progress is not a random walk. Over time, we can see patterns and structures in America's encounters with the world—both in the foreign policy of the government and when we consider the broader engagement of the nation as a whole. Security interests and economic interests have a way of making themselves felt, and American society continually tries to express certain values and ideas through its interaction with the rest of the world.

This means our grand strategy cannot be read in documents and speeches, even those emanating from senior officials. Those documents express intentions and hopes, but they only sometimes and to a limited extent describe what the United States will actually do in a given situation. The grand strategy of the United States is something that we fundamentally have to infer from the record of what we have done in the past—a project of historical scholarship and deductive reasoning, doing our best to connect the dots to see what kinds of pictures we made. Because American foreign policy is determined by so many competing forces with often contradictory agendas and different power to affect different issues, these pictures are always going to be a bit fuzzy and we will never quite settle the controversies about what the United States actually did or intended at any particular point in the past.

To move from the historical study of what our grand

strategy has been to think about what our grand strategy can or should become is to take on new realms of uncertainty. If American foreign policy is shaped in part by economic and social forces in American society beyond the control of governments and policy makers, then a view of American grand strategy must necessarily also be a view of where American society is headed: where our social, cultural, religious, technological, and economic development is taking us. To that we must add a view on how the rest of the world is changing—as a whole, and in different regions of interest to the United States. Do we like or dislike the ways in which the various elements of global society are changing, and what, if anything, can we do to further the changes we like and retard those we don't?

If my studies in American history have taught me anything, it is this: No matter what I or any other student writes, we are never going to have the "perfect foreign policy" that fully reflects a single master plan for what we should do in this world. No one, not Human Rights Watch, the CEO of Halliburton, or even the editorial board of the *Weekly Standard,* is going to clamber into the driver's seat and act like Addison's angel who, "pleas'd th' Almighty's orders to perform, rides in the whirlwind, and directs the storm."

At least not for long. There will always be contradictions, tensions, and uneasy compromises in what we do. On the whole, I think that is a good thing. The world is a complicated place and America is a complicated society. We probably need a complicated foreign policy; we certainly have one.

TWO

The Shape of American Power

When one looks back across the long sweep of American history, perhaps the most striking fact that emerges is that the United States is a global power, and has been one from earliest times. We have not always been a superpower capable of dispatching great fleets and mighty armies to every corner of the globe, but we have always kept one eye on the evolution of the global system, and our military has seen global service since the earliest years of the Republic. We have not always been the world's largest economy, much less have we always had the ability to play a major role in the evolution of the global economic and trading system, but we have always seen our trade in global terms, and we have generally tried to nudge the world along in ways that would promote economic integration, although we have not been above trying to protect domestic producers from "unfair" foreign competition. Our ideological impulses have also been global. Longfellow spoke of the first shot fired in the American Revolution as "the shot heard round the world," and Americans have always thought that both their religious and their political values should prevail throughout the world.

Why? Historically, security threats and trade interests compelled us to think globally. The British sailed across the Atlantic to burn Washington; the Japanese flew across the Pacific to bomb Pearl Harbor. Trade with Asia and Europe, as well as within our hemisphere, remains vital to our prosperity. Our global trade interests create global vulnerabilities and security interests. Thomas Jefferson sent the navy to the Mediterranean against the Barbary pirates to safeguard American trade. Commodore Perry opened up Japan partly to assure decent treatment for survivors of sunken U.S. whaling ships who washed up on its shores. The last shots fired in the Civil War were from a Confederate commerce raider attacking Union shipping in the remote waters of the North Pacific.

The global nature of our interests leads to the second most striking fact about American foreign policy over the long term: our relationship with Great Britain, the other important power that has had a global orientation throughout modern history. Historically, the United States originated as part of the British world system of empire and commerce, and for most of our history our relationship to that system was the greatest foreign policy question we faced. Great Britain was the largest market for American exports until the Second World War; its merchants and manufacturers were our greatest and most effective rivals throughout the world. The British Empire was the dominant international reality for Americans during most of our history. We had more in common with Britain than we did with any other country, and only Britain shared our interest in world order; at the same time, however, there was no other power so dangerous to us or so able to frustrate our territorial and commercial ambitions.

In the end, we worked out a very comfortable arrangement. Britain established a world order and Americans could enjoy its benefits without paying its costs. The British navy was much larger than ours, and it was Britain, not the United States, that fought nasty colonial wars and maintained the balance of power in Europe. After Britain embraced the idea of free trade in the mid-nineteenth century, Americans were able to trade throughout the British Empire, and the London financial markets provided much of the investment capital that enabled American industry to grow.

In the twentieth century, as the British system weakened and fell, the primary question in American foreign policy was what to do about it. There seemed to be three possible alternatives: we could try to prop up the British Empire; we could ignore the problem of world order and let the world go about its business while we went about ours; or we could replace Great Britain and take on the dirty, expensive job ourselves. Between the start of World War I and the start of the Cold War, we tried all three. In the end, after all else failed, we took Britain's place and built our own version of the British world system, and took on Britain's old job of acting as not quite the policeman of the world, but at least the gyroscope of world order. There were many passionate and bitter debates in the United States about whether to take on this dangerous and expensive job, but a preponderance of American opinion continues to feel that we have no alternative.

There was more. What became increasingly clear through the long and bloody twentieth century, in many ways the most shocking and barbarous episode in recorded history, was that the United States could not be just another great power playing the old games of dominance with rivals and allies. Such competition led to war, and war between great powers was no longer an acceptable part of the international system. The Americans were replacing Great Britain at a moment when the rules of the game were changing forever. The United States was going to have to attempt something that no other nation had ever accomplished—something that many theorists of international relations would swear was impossible.

Perhaps it was, but the United States was going to have to do more than build another one in the world's long succession of great empires. We were going to have to build a system that could at least potentially put an end to thousands of years of great power conflicts. We were going to have to construct a framework of power that would bring some kind of enduring peace to the whole world—in a way repeating on a global scale the kind of achievement that ancient Egypt, China, and Rome had accomplished on a regional basis.

To complicate the task a bit more, we would not be able to use some of the methods the Romans and others had used. To reduce the world's other countries and civilizations to the status of tributary provinces was beyond any military power the United States either would or could bring to bear, and the American people had neither the gifts nor the desire to rule the world in this way. The United States would have to invent new forms of association and develop a new way for sovereign states to coexist in a world of weapons of mass destruction and of prickly rivalries and hostilities among religions, races, cultures, and states.

In *The Paradox of American Power,* Joseph Nye opened an important discussion about the varieties of power that the United States brings to bear as it goes about the task of building its world order.* Nye concentrated on the difference between two types of power: hard and soft. In Nye's analysis, hard power (military and economic power) works because it can make people do what you want them to do. Soft power—cultural power, the power of example, the power of ideas and ideals—works more subtly: it makes others want what you want. In the case of the American world order, soft power upholds the

* Joseph S. Nye, *The Paradox of American Power: Why the World's Only Superpower Can't Go it Alone* (Oxford: Oxford University Press, 2002).

order because it influences others to like the American system and support it of their own free will.

These are useful distinctions, and Nye's approach will have a long future in American policy discussions, but we can press them a little further. Nye's hard power includes two quite different types of power: military and economic power. Military power might usefully be called sharp power: if you try to resist it you will feel the sharp points of bayonets pushing and prodding you in the direction you are supposed to go. Economic power is sticky power; it seduces as much as it compels. Nye's concept of soft power can also usefully be split into two elements: the sweet power of American values, culture, and policy for different foreign audiences, and what, following the Italian Marxist philosopher Antonio Gramsci, Nye refers to as "the power that comes from setting the agenda and determining the framework of a debate." Gramsci himself would call this kind of power hegemonic. Hegemonic power needs to be distinguished from sweet power both because it is more coercive than the simple power of our ideas and because, at least in the case of the American system, hegemonic power arises less from the specifically sweet aspects of American power than from the interplay of sharp, sticky, and sweet power all working together. Sharp military power serves as the solid foundation of the American system. Sticky power—a set of economic institutions and policies—attracts others into our system and makes it hard for them to leave. Sweet power—the values, ideas, and politics inherent in the system we have built—keeps them happy, and hegemonic power makes something as artificial and arbitrary, historically speaking, as the American world system since World War II look natural, desirable, inevitable, and permanent. So, at least, we hope.

SHARP POWER

Sharp power refers to military power, and it is a very practical and unsentimental thing. American military policy follows rules that would have been understandable to the Hittites or the Roman Empire. Because the military is our institution whose command structure is most like that of old-world monarchies—the president, after consultation with the Joint Chiefs, issues orders, which the military obeys—this is also where our policy looks most like something Clausewitz would have recognized and might even have approved.

Security starts at home, and since the 1823 proclamation of the Monroe Doctrine, the cardinal principle of American security policy has been to keep European and Asian powers out of the Western Hemisphere. Our half of the world was not going to be run in the old European way, if we could help it. There would be no intriguing great powers, no intercontinental alliances, and, as we became stronger and more able to insist on having our own way, no European or Asian military bases from Point Barrow, Alaska, to the tip of Cape Horn. From time to time ungrateful neighbors have resented the American power monopoly, but this does not shake the country's resolve that in military affairs, at least, it will be master in what it thinks of as its own house.

Americans have gradually come to believe that their security at home also depends on the state of Eurasia, especially the extreme eastern and western fringes of the vast supercontinent between the Bering Sea and Gibraltar, where more than half the world's people live. Like the British before us, Americans believe that if any single power (other than ourselves, who, of course, can be trusted) came to dominate either of these regions, that power would have the resources and probably also the motive to challenge our system and threaten the United States at home.

The makers of America's security policy also have had their eyes on the world's sea- and air lanes. During peacetime these are vital to our prosperity and to that of our allies; in wartime we must be able to control the sea- and air lanes to support our allies and supply our forces on other continents. Britain was almost defeated by Germany's U-boats in the world wars; in today's world of integrated markets and globally distributed production networks, any interruption of trade flows would be catastrophic. Not for sixty years has there been a serious debate in the United States about whether our navy and air force should be second to none; our only debates are over the margin of superiority necessary to secure our trade and our ability to intervene in key trouble spots.

Finally and fatefully, the United States sees the Middle East as an area of vital concern, partly because we want to secure our own oil supply, but for other reasons as well. From the American point of view, there are two potential dangers in the Middle East. First, some outside power (like the Soviet Union during the Cold War) can try to control Middle Eastern oil or at least interfere with secure supplies for the United States and its allies. Second, one country in the Middle East could take over the region and try to do the same thing. Egypt, Iran, and, most recently, Iraq have all tried and, thanks largely to U.S. policy, they all failed.

In some ways, today's challenge from Osama Bin Laden and his followers resembles other threats that the United States has faced in this region during the last sixty years. The Bin Ladenites and their allies and fellow travelers want to expel the United States from the region and build a unified, theocratic state that would control the oil resources of the Muslim Middle East. The Bin Ladenites would then use that power to consolidate their dictatorship, expand its influence throughout the Muslim world, and seek to promote their ideology and power on a global scale. The Taliban regime in Afghanistan is, so far, the world's only example of what a government would look like under Bin Ladenite influence, and the example is a horrifying one. Domestically, the Taliban state was marked by economic stagnation, political oppression, and the hideous mistreatment of women. Internationally, Afghanistan became a menace to the peace and security of the rest of the world, with tens of thousands of terrorists being trained and equipped on a growing scale. The conversion of the Middle East into this kind of theocratic terror camp, with the resources of its oil wealth available for the acquisition, development, and dissemination of weapons of mass destruction is completely unacceptable to the United States, and must clearly be resisted at all costs.

In Asia, Europe, and the Middle East the United States maintains a system of alliances and bases intended to promote stability within the affected region. Overall, the United States has just over 250,000 uniformed military members permanently stationed outside its frontiers; around 43 percent were stationed on NATO territory and around 32 percent in Japan and Korea.*
Additionally, the United States has the ability to transport significant forces to these theaters and to the Middle East should tensions rise, and it preserves the ability to control the sea-lanes and air corridors necessary to the security of its forward bases.

As part of this military grand strategy, the United States maintains the world's largest intelligence and electronic surveillance organizations. Estimated to exceed

---

* Department of Defense, Washington Headquarters Services, Directorate for Information Operations and Reports. These numbers reflect permanent stationing as of September 30, 2003, not current deployment.

$30 billion this year, the U.S. intelligence budget is larger than the total military budgets of Germany, France, and Saudi Arabia.*

Over time, there has been a distinct shift in American strategic thinking toward the need for overwhelming military superiority as the surest foundation for national security. This is partly for the obvious reasons of greater security, but it is partly also because supremacy can have an important deterrent effect. If we achieve such a degree of military supremacy that challenges seem hopeless, other states might give up trying. Security competition is both expensive and dangerous. Establishing an overwhelming military supremacy might not only go far to deter potential enemies from military attack, but it might also deter other powers from trying to match the American buildup. In the long run, this could be cheaper and safer than trying to stay just a nose in front of the pack—at least, that is what advocates of these policies maintain.

STICKY POWER

Economic or sticky power works a little differently. Sticky power isn't based on military compulsion, but it is also not based on simple coincidence of wills. The carnivorous sundew plant attracts its prey by a kind of soft power—a pleasing scent that lures insects toward its sap. But once the victim has touched the sap, it is stuck; it can't get away. This is sticky power, and that is how economic power—a type of power in which both the United States and the British Empire specialized—works.

Both Britain and America built global economic systems that attracted other countries. In Britain's case, it attracted the United States into participating in the British system of trade and investment during the nine-

* John Lumpkin, "Open-Government Advocate Seeks Disclosure of Intelligence Budget," Associated Press, June 12, 2002.

teenth century. Americans benefited from being able to trade freely throughout the British Empire, and thought twice—and more than twice—about making foreign policy choices that would cut the United States off from British investment, or freeze American goods out of British markets. America's global trade was in some sense a hostage to the British navy—we could trade freely with the world as long as we had Britain's friendship, but an interruption in that friendship would mean a financial collapse.

This meant that there was always a strong lobby in the United States against war with Great Britain. Trade-dependent New England almost seceded from the United States during the War of 1812, and at every crisis in Anglo-American relations for the next turbulent century, England could count on a strong peace lobby of merchants, bankers, and traders who would be ruined by war between the two rival English-speaking powers.

Germany's experience in World War I also shows how a system of sticky power can act as a weapon. During the long years of peace before the war, Germany was drawn into the British world trading system, and its economy became more and more trade-dependent. Industry depended on raw materials that had to be imported. Manufacturers depended on foreign markets. Wheat and beef were imported from the New World, where the vast and fertile plains of the United States and the pampas of South America produced food much more cheaply than German agriculture could do at home. By 1911, the economic interdependence was so great that many, including Norman Angell, author of *The Great Illusion*, thought that wars had become so ruinously expensive that the age of warfare was over.*

Not quite. Sticky power failed to keep World War I

* Norman Angell, *The Great Illusion: A Study of the Relation of Military Power in Nations to Their Economic and Social Advantage* (London: Heinemann, 1911).

from breaking out, but it was vital to Britain's victory. Once the war started, Britain cut off the world trade Germany had grown to depend on, while thanks to the Royal Navy the British and their allies continued to enjoy access to the rest of the world's goods. Shortages of basic materials and foods dogged Germany all during the war, and by the winter of 1917–18, Germans were seriously hungry. Meanwhile, in order to even the odds, Germany tried to cut the Allies off from world markets by the U-boat campaigns in the North Atlantic. That brought the United States into the war at a time when nothing else could have saved the Allied cause. Then, in the fall of 1918, morale in the German armed forces and among civilians collapsed, fueled by the shortages. That, not military defeat, forced the German leadership to ask for an armistice.

Currently, American policy makers hope that our sticky power can prevent any conflict with China. As China develops economically, it should gain the wealth that could one day allow it to support a military that could rival ours; it is also gaining political influence in the world. Some in both China and the United States believe that the laws of history mean that the rising power of China will someday clash with the reigning American power.

Sticky power offers a way out, and one of America's most important foreign policy priorities today is to ensure that the path of integration into the global economy is attractive enough to bring China into the system. So far, there are signs this is working. China's participation in the global economic system has helped create the greatest period of prosperity and growth in China's long history. Between 1976 and 2003, China's economy grew from an estimated $106 billion to more than $1.3 trillion. More than $450 billion in American capital has gone into China during those years.* All this

* David Hale and Lyric Hughes Hale, "China Takes Off," *Foreign Affairs* 25, no. 6 (November–December 2003): 36–53

has made China a much stronger and more self confident power with a voice in world affairs that cannot be ignored. At the same time, China now needs good relations with the United States more than ever. The Chinese economy is increasingly dependent on both imports and exports to keep its economy (and its military machine) running. Hostilities between the United States and China would cripple China's financial system, deprive its industries of their best customers, and cut China off from the imports of essential raw materials like oil and other strategic commodities.

Sticky power works both ways, though. If China cannot afford war with the United States, the United States will have an increasingly hard time breaking off commercial relations with China. In an era of weapons of mass destruction, this is probably a good thing for both sides. We shall see. Sticky power did not prevent World War I, but economic interdependence runs deeper now and it is hoped that the "inevitable" conflict between the United States and China will never take place.

Sticky power, then, is important to the American project for two reasons: it helps prevent war, and, if war comes, it helps us win. The old British system never recovered from the shocks of World War I, and with the collapse of British world power during and after World War II, Americans realized that they would have to organize the global economic system as well as take on new security responsibilities after the war's end. The world economy that the United States set out to lead had fallen very far from the peak of integration it had reached under British leadership. The triple blows of the two world wars and the Depression had ripped up the delicate webs of interconnection that had sustained the earlier system. At every turn, the measures and institutions of the British system were no longer relevant or useful. In the Cold War years, as it struggled to rebuild and improve upon the old-world system, the United States had to change both the monetary base and the legal and political framework of the economic system.

Like Britain at its peak, the United States built its sticky power on two foundations: an international monetary system and free trade. The Bretton Woods agreements of 1944 made the dollar the central currency in the global system, and while the dollar was still linked to gold at least in theory for another generation, the Federal Reserve system could increase the supply of dollars in response to economic needs; in the past the supply of gold had been determined by the rhythm of discoveries in the world's major goldfields. The result for almost thirty years was the magic combination of an expanding monetary base with price stability, and these condi tions went far to help produce the economic miracle that transformed living standards in the advanced West and in Japan. The collapse of the Bretton Woods system in August 1971 ushered in a period of economic crisis, inflation, and slow growth in the world economy; by the 1980s, however, the system was functioning almost as well as ever with a new regime of floating exchange rates in which the dollar continued to play a critical role.

The progress toward free trade and the development of an international legal and political system that supported successive waves of expansion and integration across the entire world economy is one of the great (and often unheralded) triumphs of American foreign policy in the second half of the twentieth century. Legal and economic experts, largely but not entirely from the United States or educated in its expanding university system, helped developing countries build the "invisible infrastructure" of laws and institutions that could give the necessary assurances to foreign investors and traders.

Behind all this activity and helping to make it work was the Americans' willingness to open their markets, even on a nonreciprocal basis, to exports from Europe, Japan, and the developing world. This policy, very much an element of the overall grand strategy of containing communism in part through creating a prosperous and integrated noncommunist world, also helped consolidate support around the world for the American system. The role of the dollar as a global reserve currency, along with the expansionary bias of American fiscal and monetary authorities, facilitated America's assumption of the role that became known as "the locomotive of the global economy" and "the consumer of last resort." American trade deficits stimulated production and consumption in the rest of the world, significantly increasing both the prosperity of other countries and their willingness to participate in the American system.

Opening domestic markets to foreign competitors remained one of the most controversial elements in American foreign policy during the Cold War and afterward. Companies, industrial sectors, and workers who faced foreign competition bitterly opposed the openings. Another group of critics worried about the long-term consequences of the continuing trade deficits that eventually liquidated America's international position as a net creditor and converted the United States into a net international debtor sometime during the Reagan administration—and the debt has inexorably grown ever since.

John F. Kennedy used to tell his advisers that the two things which worried him most were nuclear weapons and the payments deficit. Predictions of imminent ruin and crisis (in the value of the dollar, domestic interest rates, or both) have attended every step in the rise of this deficit since the Eisenhower administration, but the negative consequences so frequently predicted have, so far, not materialized. The result has been more like a repetition on a global scale of the conversion of financial debt to political strength pioneered by the founders of the Bank of England in 1694 and repeated a century later when, at Alexander Hamilton's instigation, the United States assumed the debt of the thirteen colonies.

In both those cases, the stock of debt was bought up by the rich and the powerful, who then acquired an interest in the maintenance of the stability of the government that guaranteed the value of the debt. Rich Englishmen supported the House of Orange against the Stuarts because they feared that a Stuart restoration would undermine the value of their holdings in the Bank of England. Where your treasure lies there shall your heart be, Scripture tells us. The propertied elites of the thirteen colonies came to support the stability and strength of the new Constitution because the value of their bonds rose and fell with the strength of the national government.

Similarly, in the last sixty years, as foreigners have acquired a greater value in the United States—government and private bonds, direct and portfolio private investments of all kinds—more and more of them have acquired an interest in maintaining the strength of the American system. A collapse of the American economy and the ruin of the dollar would do more than reduce American power and prosperity. Without their best customer, countries like China and Japan would fall into depressions of their own. Every bank, and the financial strength of every country in the world, would be shaken and probably overthrown if the United States should collapse. This is sticky power with a vengeance; debt is changed from a weakness to a strength, and other countries fear to break with us because they need our markets and own our securities. Like Samson in the temple of the Philistines, a collapsing American economy—or American power—would inflict enormous, unacceptable damage on the rest of the world.

There are problems with debt power as there are with all forms of power. Pressed too far or used recklessly, a large national debt can turn from a source of strength into a crippling liability. We have managed to persuade others to trust us with their savings to an unprecedented degree; we must now justify that faith and preserve America's unique standing in the world as the country with the best long term record of meeting its obligations as they come due.

However, assuming we manage this volatile but essential aspect of our international position, the American economic system will continue to support American power in the future as it has in the last sixty years. It not only provides the United States with the prosperity needed to underwrite its security strategy, but also complements American sharp power by reinforcing the incentives and disincentives that, combined, work to encourage other countries to accept American leadership.

SWEET POWER

Turning from hard to soft power we come first to sweet power—the power of attraction to American ideals, culture, and values that draws others around the world more or less spontaneously to support or at least accept American power and American policy.

Much of this power lies in the appeal of what others perceive to be American values. Women in much of the world, for example, see the United States as a power that advocates the rights of women at the international level while also doing a better job than most countries in the world at providing women with educational, economic, and social opportunities.

During the Cold War, American anti-imperialism was another important facet of our sweet power. The United States never built a large colonial empire of its own, and in most cases it actively pressed European states to give independence to their overseas colonies after World War II.

Political democracy and human rights are values with global appeal; to the degree that the United States is seen as supporting these values, however inconsistently and imperfectly, our sweet power grows.

Sweet power does not work like gravity: not everybody feels its power. Women in much of the world may be drawn to America's feminist streak, but many people in the world, not all of them men, find the American approach to gender relations genuinely repugnant and frightening. America's consistent anticommunism during the Cold War powerfully attracted central and eastern Europeans caught in the toils of this ruinous system; many Western European intellectuals found the American stance simplistic and embarrassing. Ronald Reagan was always more popular in Poland than in Germany and France.

When American leaders talk about the universality of human rights, Europeans thrill to the rhetoric (though they often doubt the sincerity); in other parts of the world, significant groups bridle at what they see as the cultural imperialism behind the imposition of the values and priorities of the European Enlightenment on a global political agenda. (Still others in those societies resent the resentment: they see it as an attempt by local political elites to protect their positions of privilege by disingenuous appeals to dubiously indigenous traditions.)

American culture is also part of our sweet power. Billions of people enjoy American music, movies, and television programs. Here, too, however, the effect of sweet power varies. There are many people in the world who find American popular culture immoral and vulgar, and their hatred of this culture, and their fear at the transformations it threatens to wreak in various societies around the world, makes them implacable opponents of American influence and power.

Sweet power also grows from America's role in the world. After World War II the United States worked to build a world system, and built it in ways that had broad international support. Government policy ranging from security policy to economic and trade policy to such programs as Fulbright scholarships and academic exchanges created the conditions for this global effort, but the actions of American companies, nonprofits, universities, and millions of individuals provided the real energy. Elvis Presley, Walt Disney, and Marilyn Monroe did as much to carry out this American Cold War project as John Foster Dulles and C. Douglas Dillon. Edward Deming, the productivity guru who transformed Japanese industry, had an influence nearly as great as that of Douglas MacArthur; Jack Welch of General Electric and Thomas J. Watson senior and junior of IBM had almost as much influence on the American project as Henry Kissinger and Jack Kennedy. Multinational corporations originally based in the United States extended their sales, production, and management activities around the world, recruiting talented non-U.S. citizens into their ranks and ultimately propelling the most successful into the highest levels of corporate leadership. The U.S. government did very little to bring this about, and indeed in some cases placed obstacles in the way of corporations seeking to invest overseas. Yet the activity of these companies in helping to create a multinational, multicultural workspace in a climate of equality and mutual respect was and is a critical element in the success of the American project for the free world. Universities open to foreign students and professors, menu planners at McDonald's who stumbled on, apparently, the philosopher's stone of flavor to find food appealing to six-year-olds all over the world, the Hollywood directors who perfected the car chase—all this helped define the American project and make it work.

Immigration has also been a major factor in the growth of American sweet power. Some of the immigration is temporary: the hundreds of thousands of foreign students who come to the United States to study each year. Not every foreign student goes home loving the United States, but many come away from the experience with some fondness for the country and with networks of friends and contacts here.

The experience of the millions of permanent immigrants, legal and illegal alike, in the United States is also a factor in our sweet power. The very fact that tens of millions of people around the world would like to live in the United States is powerful evidence of sweet power. The remittances that immigrants send to their families around the world and the success stories that many, though of course not all, immigrants are able to report home give people all over the world a stake in America's success and a sense of participation in American life.

Finally, the generosity with which the United States provides humanitarian assistance abroad supports our sweet power. Conventional surveys of foreign aid show the United States as one of the world's less generous powers, and indeed official development assistance as a percentage of GDP is not one of the international indicators that shows America at its best. However, as Carol C. Adelman pointed out in *Foreign Affairs*, such development assistance comprises only 17 percent of total American giving overseas, and (including remittances) 61 percent of all American assistance comes from the private sector. International giving by American foundations is now equal to about $3 billion per year.* As Adelman points out, that is almost double the giving of any of the Scandinavian countries that consistently head the list of the world's most generous countries by conventional measurements. Private giving may have more impact on foreign perceptions than government assistance.

In any case, American sweet power, though limited

* Carol C. Adelman, "The Privitization of Foreign Aid: Reassessing National Largesse," *Foreign Affairs*, 25, no. 6 (November–December 2003): 9–14.

and variable, clearly plays an important role in winning sympathy and support for American foreign policy around the world. The other form of soft power, hegemonic power, is even more complex and more important. And it is to that we now turn.

THREE

Hegemonic Power and Harmonic Convergence

When Joseph Nye invoked Antonio Gramsci's concept of hegemony to explain American soft power, he was bringing one of the most important intellectual advances of the twentieth century into the discussion of American foreign policy. Struggling to understand why capitalism so obstinately refused to fulfill Marxist predictions of its imminent demise, Western communists like Gramsci were increasingly impressed with the power of "bourgeois" concepts like parliamentary democracy to win the active support of workers who, according to communist analysis, should be able to see through the flimsy hypocrisy of the bourgeois politicians. (The possibility that the workers recognized that communism was a recipe for social, moral, and economic disaster could not, of course, be entertained for a moment.)

While this line of thought never enabled Western communists to overcome the workers' obstinate attachment to property, liberty, and democracy, it did lead to a much richer understanding of the ways in which social and political orders rest on consent, and on how that consent can be built.

Like the kinds of national social orders that Gramsci and his heirs analyzed, the international order that the

United States has built since World War II is stronger, more effective, and less vulnerable to the degree that people around the world consent to it and consider this order to be legitimate and inevitable.

The power that both creates and flows from this consent is America's hegemonic power. This is not simply sweet power; people do not consent to the American system only because, and to the degree that, they like it. They also consent to it because they see it as inevitable, rooted in military power, technological prowess, broad historical development or economic power that cannot be challenged. There may be more specific reasons for consenting to the American order. The citizens of a small state like Singapore might consent to the order because they believe that the American world order is the best way to secure the prosperity and independence of a rich city state in, potentially, a dangerous neighborhood. Others might not like the American system very much, but if the system seems strongly rooted, they may decide that resistance is too expensive and the outcome too uncertain. Their best choice is to exploit whatever opportunities the system affords.

Sharp, sticky, and sweet power all contribute to hegemonic power and, as they work together, these three different types of power lose their specific identity to come together synergistically and create a whole that is greater than the sum of its parts.

Take the American military. It is a gross oversimplification to say that military power operates only as sharp or even as hard power. The U.S. military has created a historically unique network of military-to-military ties embracing almost every country in the world. Officers from all over the world come to the United States to train in our staff colleges or use our equipment. American standards of training are often considered a kind of gold standard in militaries all over the world, and participation in advanced seminars and exercises with the American military can materially assist the careers of foreign officers. NATO expansion, perhaps the most significant accomplishment of the Clinton administration, saw this soft side of military power deployed as armed forces created by communist regimes to oppose the United States made the transition to democratic armed forces in alliance with it. Military strength has been part of an overall strategy that combined sharp, sticky, and sweet power to create durable new power relationships and root them in strong institutions in the ten short years after the fall of the Soviet Union.

Another synergistic exercise of power can be seen in the Middle East. The identification of the Middle East and its oil resources as a vital American interest to be protected if necessary at the cost of war is often seen by opponents of the American system as a classic example of the cynical and heartless character of American power. "No Blood for Oil" read signs at marches protesting both the first and second Gulf wars against Iraq.

In fact, the American objectives in the Middle East are much further reaching. The United States is less interested in feeding its oil thirst and in gaining contracts for powerful energy-sector companies than it is in the impact of oil security—or insecurity—on world politics as a whole. Because the United States has both the power and the will to maintain the security of the oil trade, other countries see no adequate reason to develop their own independent military capabilities to secure their oil supplies. A world with half a dozen great powers dueling for influence in the Middle East, with each power possessing the will and the ability to intervene with military force in this explosive region, would be a less safe and less happy world than the one we now live in, and not only for Americans. Providing the "international public good" of a secure oil supply not only helps ensure *America's* oil supply, it helps make the United States the lone global superpower in a world of regional powers, and it also reinforces the widespread (though by no means universal) belief that American power helps underwrite and secure world peace. And, of course, at the same time, the other world powers know that there is one country that has the ability to interrupt the world's oil flows should it feel the need to do so. Here, the sharp power of military supremacy has helped create both the sticky power that the world's integrated energy market provides the United States and the sweet power that flows from the reduction of international military competition under the *Pax Americana*.

What may be the most important element of American hegemonic power has its roots in America's domestic political economy during the first two thirds of the twentieth century. During those years America's key domestic project was to build a new social system. Based on a combination of mass production and mass consumption, the United States was able to build a new kind of economy, prosperity, and democracy. That system and the vision of history behind it would become America's most important export during the Cold War, and has shaped America's influence in the world.

Marxist critics described this American economic model during most of the twentieth century as the "Fordist" system, naming it after Henry Ford, who first developed the combination of organized mass production and high wages (so that his workers could buy the Model T cars they produced) that lay at the heart of the new American domestic system.

To make Fordism work, as Americans discovered through the middle of the twentieth century, a host of political, economic, and social changes and policies were needed.

The traditional American preference for laissez-faire government weakened because the long investment cycle of the new industrial corporations needed macroeconomic stability, with governments supporting purchasing power in good times and bad. The deep-seated hostility of the American legal system to organized labor was modified to allow and even encourage unionization, while preventing the rise of anticapitalist labor movements or labor that disputed the right of management to organize the work process. American society underwent a whole range of cultural changes to support mobility and mass consumption, the lifestyles required by the new economy. The anarchic, cutthroat capitalism of earlier American eras gave way to a more stable system in which a handful of large companies with large labor unions peaceably divided the mass market. There were three broadcasting networks, one phone company, basically three car companies, two major bus companies, and so on. Banks, airlines, and utilities were tightly regulated.

Fordist society was an administered society. As many sociologists observed at the time, the nature of business organizations had changed. The old division of society into owner-entrepreneurs on the one hand and blue-collar workers (and poorly paid clerks) on the other had yielded to a new kind of society in which a large class of relatively well paid white-collar managers ran regulated, major corporations along bureaucratic lines.

Fordist politics was also administrative. The progressive reformers of the late nineteenth and early twentieth centuries had campaigned to take politics out of government as far as possible. The patronage appointees of the old spoils system were increasingly replaced by a professional civil service with life tenure. With the role of politicians shrinking, government was to be conducted along objective, scientific principles as revealed by the new social sciences.

The new civil servants managed an ever-growing state involvement in the economy as large-scale investments in electricity, highways, and other forms of infrastructure seemed too large and too risky to be left to private enterprise. In an age of universal suffrage, this system was a way of reconciling democratic politics with the need of the state to manage sophisticated enterprises that average voters and elected officials did not appreciate or understand. Progressives reasoned that corrupt political machines and their retinues of semi-educated office seekers could not manage the complex problems of twentieth-century society.

Public and private managers were trained in a vastly expanded educational establishment that provided training and employment for the intellectuals who once sat in shabby cafés earnestly plotting the overthrow of an iniquitous system; they would find comfortable, well-paying jobs within Fordist society.

A chicken in every pot, a car in every garage, and an angel in every whirlwind—that was the Fordist ambition. Fordist society would be prosperous, stable, safe, and well guided by administrators and engineers trained to make objective and rational decisions in the common good. Instead of a class struggle between workers and capitalists, it would be based on a compromise.

The capitalist class accepted government limits on its economic and social power. The great corporations had to work within a framework of antitrust laws. The rich had to accept that regulated financial markets would limit their ability to use financial maneuvers to build vast personal business empires without regard for the rights and interests of others. Progressive income taxes and heavy inheritance taxes limited the ability of capitalists to accumulate and pass on great personal wealth. On the other hand, capitalists were assured that the majority of noncapitalist voters would respect private property and the basic requirements of a capitalist system. The regulation of the economy might limit the flexibility of big companies, but it protected them from aggressive start-up rivals, and also assured them a positive macroeconomic environment as the government used its financial power to prevent the costly and dangerous depressions of earlier eras.

On the other hand, workers gave up the utopian dreams of equality and worker control that communism promised—a concession made easier because the actual experience of the "workers' states" was so murderous and grim. Work in the Fordist world was usually hard, monotonous, and under the rigid control of supervisors and timetables. On the other hand, it was much better paid than ever before, and workers were assured gradual improvements in their standard of living.

The broker of the Fordist class compromise, and perhaps its biggest winner, was the class Karl Marx and, after him, the hard-nosed revolutionaries of the communist movement most despised, although it was also the class from which most of the communist leadership sprang: the petite bourgeoisie, especially its administrative and managerial elements rather than its entrepreneurial groups of small businessmen.

Society's intellectuals, administrators, and managers offered themselves to capitalists and workers as the "honest brokers" who could resolve the clashes and competing ambitions of the capitalist whirlwind, the disinterested angels who could ride the vortex and direct the storm. They could find technical solutions to the economic and social disputes that threatened to disrupt the cooperation and stability on which the complex machine of modern capitalist society depended for its success. The social sciences—Keynesian economics, the new forms of practical, "post-ideological" sociology, psychology, education, and penology—discovered and put into practice by the heroic social engineers of the Fordist petite bourgeoisie would guide human society toward the rational utopia of the European Enlightenment through a gradual and peaceful process of progress.

The ideological competition between the United States and the Soviet Union during the Cold War was in large part a competition between Fordism and communism. Fordism, Americans and their allies proclaimed, gave ordinary people more affluence, more personal freedom, and more political equality and democracy than communism could. Combining the dynamism of markets with the stabilizing effects of government macroeconomic policy and ever more lavish social safety nets, Fordist economies escaped the fate that communists had predicted. They neither destroyed themselves in economic crises and depressions nor created a rebellious, "immiserated" proletariat that overthrew a hated system in sheer, desperate self-defense.

There was something else: As the *Pax Americana* became established after World War II the capitalist countries no longer tore themselves apart in recurring wars. The first half of the twentieth century was a sickening period in world history, with hundreds of millions killed in waves of war and political violence. Communists made great strides exploiting the misery and instability resulting from these wars; they also used the fear of war as an effective tool of propaganda. The need of giant corporations for ever-larger markets, exacerbated by the special greed of arms manufacturers, they claimed, meant that capitalist societies were driven inevitably toward conflict and war.

Fordism provided the United States with a persuasive argument that capitalism was better than communism at bringing peace to the world. Since 1945 there have been no wars among the large capitalist countries; international conflicts have moved from the center to the periphery of the capitalist world, with wars fought either against communist expansion (for example in the Korea and Vietnam conflicts), among developing countries, or against peripheral rogue states like Iraq. Since 1945, the major capitalist countries have also been increasingly free of scourges like fascism and autocracy. The long, prosperous, and democratic peace in post-1945 Europe was a powerful argument for the American system among

peoples who had suffered through thirty years of horror
between 1914 and 1945.

Mid-century America came to propound a view of history that we can call the doctrine of harmonic convergence. Descended from and claiming to fulfill the hopes
of the European Enlightenment, recognizably related to
Marxist ideas of progress, and resonating with traditional
American optimism, the concept of harmonic convergence was the spearhead of capitalism in its ideological
war with communism and also a key element in winning
widespread world consent to the American system.

The ideas of harmonic convergence are reasonably
simple and to many the implications remain attractive.
Capitalism raises living standards by promoting technological growth and the efficient use of resources. Over
time, this creates the social wealth for universal education and mass affluence. As education spreads, bigotry
and superstition fade. An educated workforce is more
productive; a benign cycle of rising productivity and rising living standards gives society the wealth to establish
ever more generous welfare states without depriving the
rich and the successful of the incentives which lead them
to invest and create. Trade makes societies culturally
cosmopolitan as contact between them increases; the
spread of democracy makes the world more peaceful and
more culturally homogenous.

From Rockefeller Republicans to Acheson Democrats,
the American establishment of the era saw this as a
domestic as well as an international transformation. The
dreams of the progressive movement would be gradually
attained. As capitalism developed and America became
more advanced, the country would become more cosmopolitan and progressive. We would be more like Western
Europe: post-historical, secular, with a social welfare
state. We would be more intellectually meritocratic, less
driven culturally by the mix of popular taste and entre-

preneurialism. The values of the educated, liberal, and progressive social engineers would replace the values of the "great unwashed."

Progress meant the rise of the rational and the retreat of the irrational forces in human nature and, therefore, in human history. Fundamentalism would vanish; mainstream versions of the Protestant, Catholic, and Jewish religious traditions would converge under the gradual progress of enlightenment; our sense of nationalism would also become more "civilized" and nuanced. Fordist America would be the fulfillment of the dream of the European Enlightenment.

Not the least potent attractor for foreign opinion in the Fordist vision for the world was the way in which its logic predicts that American power would increasingly become kinder, gentler and less arbitrary. Already Fordism was bringing order to the jungle of capitalist competition as regulation and order replaced savage competition. Similarly, the *Pax Americana* would progressively tame the jungles of international politics. The network of institutions would thicken; the rules of law and multilateral cooperation would replace the savage struggles for power and primacy that formerly characterized international life.

The *Pax Fordiana* promised a bright future for Europe. Economic logic and the experience of history suggested that over time European economies would catch up to the United States in productivity and output. As U.S. relative economic power declined, we would carry out our foreign policy through increasingly dense networks of institutions and sovereignty would be something to pool rather than something to jealously preserve. Our international life like our capitalism at home would become less like a jungle and more like a garden party. There would be more stability, more regulation, and more equality in the distribution of its rewards.

A Fordist world is a world of strong and stable institutions—within nations and including nations. During the Cold War, this vision of the future looked realistic. From 1949 to 1989, alliances were stable and international relations in general were slow to change. Institutions whose processes were slow and which presupposed largely unchanging political relationships and allegiances among their member states were seen as capable forums for responding to various challenges that might arise. In the Fordist view of the future, the institutions were supposed to proliferate and strengthen their mandates. Just as the disinterested administration by trained personnel was supposed to replace the hurly burly of politics and patronage in domestic governmental affairs in the progressive utopia, international politics were also to pass into the realm of cooperation, administration and law. The EU with its growing powers in Brussels was seen as the leading edge of the way international life is evolving. The United Nations would gradually, inevitably gain power as the harmonic convergence proceeds.

This vision of harmonic convergence is central to the idea of progress as most of the west has understood it since the defeat of European fascism. During most of the twentieth century, this vision of the future was also predominant in the United States, and it went hand in glove with the Fordist tendency to substitute a more regulated, smoother form of administered capitalism in Progressive America than the rough nineteenth-century version.

It also vastly eased the task of American foreign policy by suggesting that the elements of American politics and culture that complicate its message will gradually fade. This vision of harmonic convergence presents a view of the historical process that made it much easier for the United States to win friends overseas. Time was on the side of the social system the United States was defending, and time would also domesticate the United States.

American exceptionalism was expected to become a thing of the past. American Jacksonians would wither away; Archie Bunker may die unrepentantly waving an American flag, but Gloria and Meathead will live in John

Lennon's utopia: "Nothing to kill or die for, and no religion too." Their children will probably use the metric system. The features of the world system that looked like an American empire were temporary, passing phenomena: when the end of history finally came, the empire would dissolve into a liberal, Fordist order and peaceful, cosmopolitan administrators would arbitrate the conflicts of mankind.

Fordism and a security blanket: this was a great system for America to be in the business of exporting. While there was plenty of resistance to it from traditionalists and fascists on the right and from communists and socialists on the left, Fordism in time proved to be the definitive solution to many of Europe's most vexing problems. Wars between nations and the struggle between classes had convulsed European history for generations; after 1945 it became increasingly clear that the new dispensation could solve both of these problems. Elites had to give up some of their national independence and pride in Europe and Japan, but American power kept the communists at bay. The working classes had to give up the ideology of class struggle and accept capitalism as a way of life, but they were clearly living better than ever before.

Fordism choked Marxism (and fascism) with butter; the combination of abundance and opportunity in Western Europe and Japan cemented the alliances that won the Cold War and steadily undermined the faith of the communist elites in their own system. From the standpoint of Western Europe's increasingly frustrated communist intellectuals, the success of Fordism consolidated the hegemony of "bourgeois democracy" in postwar Europe. In much the same way, the success of Fordist policies and the international appeal of the vision of a harmonically convergent historical process toward a peaceful and prosperous law-bound world order helped make it seem credible that the postwar international system established by American power was a progressive advance for the whole world and not just for the United States.

In the first world, limited national independence (subordination in the American system of alliances; acceptance of Washington's economic and political dominance) was offset by mass prosperity and enhanced security. In the third world, limited prosperity was offset by enhanced national independence and a development model that promoted political stability by enhancing the ability of national governments to shape economic development and distribute patronage and rewards.

In the third world, America did not ask much of elites, and most of them were happy to join the American coalition against a communism that threatened their power and privileges. And while in many cases the masses in the developing world were excluded and marginalized by the economic system, the satisfaction of national pride that came from expelling the hated European overlords was a glue that could hold society together. Also, the strategies popular during most of the Cold War and recommended by the World Bank at the time called for elite-guided large development projects and a state-controlled credit system, so economic development acted to reinforce the political power of the country's leadership. Who got a dam, who got a steel mill, who got access to foreign exchange, who got the formal-sector jobs in the civil service and state-owned industrial sector, who got access to the housing program: under the mid-century development model these decisions were given to local elites who had reason to accept the American system, even as they continued to denounce the "neocolonial" Americans and their exploitative ways.

As the Soviet Union crumbled before the triumphant power of the American system in the late 1980s, Americans believed they had built an enduring order. As former director of policy planning in the U.S. State Department Francis Fukuyama famously notes in *The End of History and the Last Man,* liberal capitalist democracy was an enduring social system because it met human needs in ways that no alternative could match. This was a vision of harmonic convergence buttressed by Hegelian dialectics, and for most American policy makers—even when they were not consciously thinking of the system as a whole—harmonic convergence *was* the American project.

For many Americans, including much of our foreign policy establishment, this version of the American project for the world, evolving in response to the stresses and dangers of the twentieth century, needs no defense. It is much more than a way of defending ourselves in a dangerous world; the American project is a distinguished moral initiative. It promises to usher in—and for hundreds of millions if not billions of people it already has—a world of unprecedented security, freedom, and affluence.

As the friends of the American project contemplate its history, even they must concede that there have been errors and unfortunate occurrences. (Others prefer the term "crimes.") During the Cold War, Americans too often supported dictatorial regimes in exchange for support against the Soviet Union. The United States has not always chosen wisely when and how to intervene in other countries. Hundreds of thousands died in the Rwanda genocide because we failed to act; more died in Indochina because we acted unwisely. The benefits of *Pax Americana* have been distributed very unevenly; Europe, Japan, North America, and parts of South and East Asia may be richer than at any time in world history, but real, inflation-adjusted GDP per person in many African countries is lower than it was at the time these countries became independent. The development advice from American economists and the international financial institutions has had, to put it mildly, mixed consequences in the developing world. The industrialization of the third world has repeated on a larger scale the crimes and miseries that first occurred in Europe and North America during the first industrial revolution. Unfair trade and investment policies have placed obstacles in the paths of poor countries. The chaotic rush for development that has characterized the capitalist process under American tutelage has caused vast social and environmental damage.

All of this has led a significant and vocal minority in the United States to condemn the American project in whole or in part. Outside the United States this sentiment is more widespread still and in much of the world constitutes a majority verdict on the history of the American project.

Yet Americans by and large remain proud of this history, and sought little more after the Cold War than to go forward in much the same way. The broad consensus view in the United States was that while the collapse of the Soviet Union might create a few complications, notably in the Balkans and the Caucasus, on the whole the task facing the United States after the Cold War was a simpler version of the American project: to build a world of free markets and free governments under the aegis of American military might—and to build that world without significant opposition.

The four types of American power—sharp, sticky, sweet, and hegemonic—seemed as strong or stronger than ever after the collapse of the Soviet Union removed the only full-scale military challenge to American might and discredited the only serious alternative social model to the American system. In the post–Cold War world the convergence would accelerate and the harmonies would deepen; that is what most Americans expected. September 11 is what they got.

PART TWO

The Gathering Storm

FOUR

Faulty Towers

Americans like to think of themselves as a sunny and optimistic people and it always surprises and grieves us to learn that other countries are sometimes incapable of appreciating the true beauty of the world system Americans are trying to build. China, Russia, France, and Iran, for example, have serious misgivings about American power and American intentions, and they are not alone. But the problems that come from outside the system in some ways are easier both to understand and to deal with than problems that come from within. If the opponents of the American system ever succeed in bringing it down, their success is likely to come from exploiting the inner weaknesses and contradictions of the American strategy rather than defeating American arms in the field.

One of these contradictions has to do with the dual nature of America's role in the world. On the one hand, the United States sees itself, accurately, as the chief agent in a global revolutionary process through which liberal capitalism and liberal democracy are sweeping the world. Where these values do not yet exist, American society and to some degree the American government seek change. We press China to become more democratic, Europe and Japan to embrace more liberal versions of capitalism, and the Muslim Middle East to do both. American power brings change, uncomfortable change, and naturally others resist it.

At the same time, as a balance-seeking, hegemonic, and order-building power, the United States has a conservative dimension to its thinking. We may want the system to change, but we also want it to stay the same—to be stable. We do not want to push reform in Saudi Arabia so hard that we destabilize a key ally. We are at least as interested in maintaining a conservative balance of power in Asia as we are in persuading China to give Tibet more autonomy. Frequently, the American revolutionary projects threaten the interests of various governments important to regional or global stability. Americans are rarely able to solve these problems elegantly.

If the United States were simply a conservative power in world affairs, like China, Egypt, and other empires of old, the fall of the Berlin Wall might have signaled, as so many hoped, the end of history.

American power is, however, inextricably bound up with the fortunes of the capitalist economic system, and capitalism is not a stable and placid social system. It no sooner reaches maturity in one phase than it begins to move on, driven unpredictably but dynamically by changes in technology, institutions, and practices.

This is not something that anybody can stop or control in a capitalist framework, even though the short- and medium-term consequences are not always pleasant. Important aspects of the international crises following September 11 were simply the result of progress. The rapid technological progress that capitalism fosters is making weapons of mass destruction easier and cheaper to make. In 1945 it took the world's greatest industrial power and an international consortium of the world's most brilliant scientists to make the first nuclear weapons. Today, a country like Pakistan, badly governed, economically backward, and unable to enforce the reign of law through its own territories, can build nuclear weapons using local scientists of no great accomplishment or renown. It does not take much imagination to project these trends ahead; more and more terrifying weapons are going to be cheaper and easier to produce.

As progress makes these terrible weapons easier to manufacture, it also undermines the efficacy of international cooperation for nonproliferation. As the materials and technology of nuclear destruction become more widespread and easier to make, it is harder and harder for sanctions and inspections to stop countries determined to build these weapons. It is also harder to know what stage countries are at in their efforts to build nuclear weapons; the United States was surprised by the nuclear tests in both India and Pakistan, and North Korea cheated undetected on its 1994 agreement with the United States.

Without the technological progress spurred on and accelerated by the triumph of capitalism, we would have no crisis over terrorism and weapons of mass destruction. Without progress, the United States would not increasingly face the wrenching choice of acting unilaterally against proliferators or allowing states with ties to terrorists to acquire nuclear weapons.

Bad as things are, we are nowhere near the climax of this roller coaster ride. As the international capitalist system Americans have worked so hard to build continues to reward innovation, we can expect the increasingly rapid development of new technologies, especially in biology, that can unleash unimaginable destruction with relative ease. As more and more countries achieve more and more prosperity, the number of scientists and laboratories in the world will continue to grow even more rapidly than world population as a whole. These scientists will have access to ever-more sophisticated (and cheaper) equipment and ever-faster access to information about the efforts of other teams of researchers around the world. With more and more capital available in more and more efficient capital markets, inventors will get backing for promising new techniques more and more quickly.

Our victories and achievements create the next set of challenges we must face. This is inherent in the nature of American power and of the social system we exemplify and seek to build. Fatuous reflections on unipolarity and triumphalist self-congratulation on the victory of free market capitalism should never blind us to the revolutionary nature of the American project and the appalling nature of the threats (balanced, one hopes, by the blessings) that accelerating technological progress unleashes on the world. The American project isn't something that we accomplish once and for all; history isn't something that we bring to an end. Rather, each generation of Americans must reinvent its country and its foreign policy to meet the demands of a world that, thanks in large part to our own success, is perpetually more complex and more explosive.

Another major and unavoidable source of tension is the contradiction between what the United States is and what it is trying to do. The age-old contest of nations for dominion and conquest has filled the world with blood and, under the conditions of modern warfare, might wipe out mankind if it continues. The United States wants this history to end, but in practice that means we have had to clamber to the top of the greasy pole and now must defend our position. Are we winning the game or ending it? Are we creating a world order or conquering the world? Inevitably, we find ourselves doing a good bit of both, and it is not always easy to manage the tension between the two strategies.

Foreigners can and do look with alarm at the way America defines and seeks its goals in the world. They look at the way ethnic lobbies have influenced U.S. foreign policy and ask themselves if putting the American political system in charge of the planet is really the best way to go. As the U.S. military budget passes $400 billion a year, foreigners see our military power growing past any constraint and they worry how we might behave in a world in which we felt no checks on our power. Democracies as well as dictatorships have reasons to suspect and even oppose American power. While populism has been a less potent factor in European foreign policy than it has been in the United States in recent years, the populations of democratic countries in Europe, for example, are still used to living in societies in which public opinion affects foreign policy, and are in the habit of thinking that their opinions influence world affairs. Many Europeans were painfully shocked, during the preparations for the American invasion of Iraq, to discover just how little the United States government at times can care about public opinion among people who do not vote in American elections. From the standpoint of many people around the world, an increase in American power means a *decrease* in global democracy: 300 million people who live in the United States are getting more say; the 6.3 billion people who live in the rest of the world are getting less.

The American system faces two dangers. If the United States accumulates or uses too little power, the American system may fall apart as others pick away at it. Accumulate too much power, or use it in too heavy-fisted a way, and the system may disintegrate as others combine against it.

There is no way to solve this problem once and for all. What the United States tried to do during most of post–World War II history was to exercise its power as a liberal hegemon, maximizing the degree of consent and consultation with others without neglecting the need for strong American power underwriting the world system. We do not want to be perpetually imposing our will at gunpoint, but we also do not want to live in a world in which the United States cannot act without permission from a majority of other countries.

Setting up and working within international institutions is one of the most important but also one of the most problematic ways in which the United States has tried to manage the tensions between the imperial and cooperative aspects of its world role. For the United States, international institutions are important because they can build stronger and more effective coalitions to attack important international problems—we value them to the degree that they enhance our ability to advance our global and national interests while sharing costs and responsibilities with other countries. They also enhance American power because the decisions of the "international community" are widely seen as more acceptable and legitimate than American mandates. By giving other countries real influence, and sometimes control, over decisions that are important to them, institutions can also reduce the international unhappiness about America's global supremacy. For all these reasons, international institutions have been central to American policy making for decades.

Unfortunately, international institutions are not a magic solution that can fully resolve the tensions of the American world role. They can sometimes cause serious problems. International institutions include countries who do not share America's sense of values and priorities. This can mean countries like China who do not accept the American view of democracy. It can also mean countries that are hostile to American power, or countries who believe that the international system should be acting more aggressively to curb American power and subject it more fully to the rule of law.

There are two groups of countries in the world today who simply do not agree with the American vision of world order, and who therefore often have fundamental differences with the United States over issues ranging from the role of institutions in international life to the specific policies and priorities that the international community should adopt at various moments. One of these groups takes the ideas of the harmonic convergence to their logical extreme and wants the international system to move rapidly towards a purely legal and administrative framework in which American power, like the power of all countries, will be checked and limited by sovereign international institutions. The progressive imagination of the twentieth century saw international politics emerging from a chaotic, hellish past of great power rivalry and climbing laboriously toward an imagined future heaven where might would be firmly subordinated to right and world government would put an end to war.

In today's international politics, the "Party of Heaven" is often represented by countries like Germany and Canada. These countries believe that heaven is within our grasp if we would just reach out for it, and that if the United States would submit its power to international institutions, the world would be well on the way toward permanent peace. They seek to thicken the network of international institutions to cover more and more issues that were once handled politically and to give existing institutions greater powers over individual states, especially the United States. For these countries, international institutions are a world government in waiting, and they don't want the wait to be long.

The other group includes countries like Russia and France. These countries still think in terms of traditional power politics, and they generally believe that American power needs to be kept in check. They are realists in foreign policy and generally have little patience with idealistic dreamers and their fantasies of professional, impartial world government. Their diplomats are likely to roll their eyes and sidle towards the exit when earnest Canadians buttonhole them to lobby for tougher global regulations against cruelty to animals, and they believe that international relations will always ultimately revolve around power. This might look like the "Party of Hell" from the standpoint of those who want effective and powerful international institutions, but Heaven and Hell can sometimes agree—usually on the importance of international institutions to limit American power.

From an American standpoint, it is hard to say who is more annoying: the partisans of heaven or those of the other place. Russia, France, and the other old-fashioned powers would like to dismantle the American hegemony, however liberal it becomes, and see the world system revert to the old anarchic habits of multipolar competition. As they look to their own national interests and resist the accumulation of additional power by the United States, these countries spend a lot of time looking for ways to isolate the United States, harass and undermine the world system, and generally make trouble for American policy makers.

The Party of Heaven can be just as frustrating. Washington believes that strengthening American national power is the best way to strengthen the peaceful American international system that represents the closest thing to heaven planet earth is likely to experience anytime soon. When Germans or Canadians lecture Americans over Washington's unwillingness to give up more power to multilateral institutions, American policy makers can feel like an ambulance driver rushing to an accident scene who is pulled over and lectured by an officious policeman about speeding. Victims may be dying, but the policeman still has a lecture to deliver, and the ambulance cannot proceed until every word of the speech has been heard.

Too often for Washington's comfort, the two parties combine. The Party of Hell is cynical about the ability of international institutions to manage the conflicts of real life, while at the same time the members of this party have no intention of piously respecting international systems when they are established. But they think that establishing the institutions can weaken and hobble the United States, or that if America opposes the extension and improvement of the institutions it will lose influence and friends as its hegemony looks less liberal and alluring.

The Party of Heaven thinks institutions can, if strengthened, replace old fashioned foreign policy, and this party resists American attempts to preserve its freedom of action. If the United States tries to negotiate compromises in, say, the charter for the International Criminal Court in ways that would protect American officials and military from abuses of the court's authority, the Party of Heaven cries that the United States is "weakening" and "watering down" important institutions. The Party of Hell joins in, gleefully and hypocritically. The United States ends up frequently caught in a damaging crossfire between the forces of darkness and the armies of light. The two parties have diametrically opposed visions of the world, and could never develop together a constructive alternative to the American project, but they can and often do agree to form a purely negative coalition to block or at least perplex the United States.

Truthfully, neither of the parties has a very logical position. The Party of Heaven essentially demands that the United States embark on military action only with the approval of the Security Council. Since France, Russia and China have vetoes there, this position means that a non-democratic country like China, or believers in old fashioned power politics like Russia and France can block actions that threaten their interests. The Party of Heaven's position means putting the Party of Hell in charge. A Security Council on which Germany, Canada, Denmark, Sweden, and Vatican City held the permanent, veto-wielding seats might logically command the support of the Party of Heaven. In its current form, the Security Council stands for the permanent veto of expediency over principle, of national interest over the common purpose of the human race.

The other party is just as inconsistent. Russia and France can and do argue that they have a legitimate right to use all available tools to defend their national interest against the dangerous and growing power of the United States. Fair enough, and all of history and common sense is on their side. Yet if the game is dirty power politics rather than high-minded international law, the United States has the right to play, too. If countries like France and Russia have the right to oppose and limit American power, the United States has an equal right to use its power and influence to reduce the power of its rivals. In the old world of power politics, power can only be bound by power, not by fine words and paper treaties. If Russia and France are right about the way the world works, the United States has the right and even the duty to ignore the Security Council from time to time.

The basic American position—that institutions like the Security Council are an important element of international relations, but that they cannot bear the full weight that the Party of Heaven would like to place on them—is the one which best accords with historical realities and the necessities as well as the aspirations of world order. Yet logic is of little help in the political difficulties that the two parties can often create when they combine against the United States.

Very often, the United States has no good choices in these situations. Whatever it chooses to do, a price will be paid. Legalities and formalities *can* reduce the effectiveness of American power; unilateralism and arbitrary action *can* undermine the cooperation necessary for a healthy world system. We will inevitably make the wrong choice sometimes; inevitably, also, the price even for a right choice may be higher than we can comfortably pay. Again, we can manage this tension more or less well; we cannot resolve or end it. It is inherent in the nature of America's world role.

Inevitably, too, these problems have an irritating way of surfacing at moments of crisis. Russia tried to use its veto against the American position in the Balkans at the height of the Kosovo crisis; the crisis over Iraq gave

France a heaven-sent opportunity to lead a global charge against the United States. Hard as it may be for narcissistic American policy makers to recognize the fact, not everybody in the world thinks American power is a good thing. Nor do nations such as France and Russia identify America's interests with some kind of general international good. A crisis, when the United States needs the institutions to work well, is just the moment when others see a heaven- or hell-sent opportunity to delay, harass, and hinder American policy.

FIVE

The Decline of Fordism and
the Challenge to American Power

Talking about stages of capitalism is a difficult business. Over time, however, it is clear that capitalism has existed in somewhat different forms. In its very early stages, European capitalism rose in a world still dominated by feudalism and was mostly confined to a handful of merchants and producers, while the great majority of the population continued to live as, at best, free peasants in a near-feudal economy where money was rare and profit was hardly a concept.

The industrial revolution unleashed another stage in capitalist history. One can call this the era of Victorian capitalism. It was the time of Oliver Twist and William Blake's "dark satanic mills." Workers were brutally exploited, and competition between capitalists was fierce and unstinting. Frequent financial upheavals and panics sent waves of bankruptcy through the ranks of entrepreneurs and investors; bitter class struggles over wages and working conditions increasingly influenced politics. State regulation of industry was limited, and capitalists were largely free to do what they pleased without oversight of any kind. This is the system that Marx predicted would someday be overthrown by impoverished workers, but as we have seen it gave rise instead to Fordism.

The capitalism of the Fordist era was kinder, gentler,

and more predictable than its Victorian predecessor, and as was discussed, its heyday accompanied and facilitated the establishment of the American system after World War II. The trouble is that capitalism did not stop with Henry Ford and the system named for him. The era of regulation, income equality, state planning, and stability has gradually been yielding to a new form of capitalism over the last generation.

Many writers have worked to describe the difference between Fordism and what we might as well call "millennial capitalism," the new system we seem to be inventing and exploring. For some, the shift from Fordism to millennialism is a rake's progress: the end of a system that produced peace, justice, mass prosperity, and social security and the rise of a grotesque new system of inequality, instability, and bare-knuckled competition in a hideous, neoliberal dog-eat-dog world. For others, the shift represents the glorious triumph of technology and entrepreneurial spirit over a decadent and stagnant era, and the new and more dynamic capitalism offers opportunities to eliminate poverty and transform the human condition.

Both views, of course, are partly true. Most observers seem to agree that Ronald Reagan and Margaret Thatcher were the first political leaders who set about the conscious destruction of Fordism in the interest of a new, more vigorous form of capitalism. It is not yet and may never be clear exactly why the shift occurred when and as it did; many analysts point to the rise of unregulated, offshore "Eurodollar" markets in the late 1960s and early 1970s as the economic beginning of the transition. The rise of computer technology played a major role by making financial markets infinitely more sophisticated and complex than ever before; the growth of international trade from the very low levels following the disruptions of the Great Depression and World War II was also a factor.

In any case, for much of the last generation, economic

practices and institutions that were once seen as pillars of a successful economy have been increasingly considered obstacles to progress. Labor unions, state ownership of key companies, and state-guided investment strategies— building blocks of Fordism—have come under increasing attack around the world.

The globalization of production has played an increasing role in the breakdown of the Fordist model. From a system in which a handful of national companies presided placidly over stable markets, distributing the rents of oligopoly to unionized workers and shareholders while docile, slow-moving banks made low-risk loans to captive customers, we have moved to a volatile system of global competition. Jobs and whole industries rise and vanish within a few years. The progress of capital is destroying the Fordist economy and the political and international systems that rose with it.

This phenomenon, which I first wrote about twenty years ago in *Mortal Splendor: The American Empire in Transition*, after a shaky start has given the American economy a new burst of growth and contributed to the climate of confidence and invulnerability of the lost years. Although the transition was a bitter one for many people in the United States, and much of the public would like, if possible, to reverse the decades of change, the new capitalism remains much more popular inside the United States than in most places outside it.

Here I have to ask readers to indulge me. The transformation of capitalism in the last twenty years is a subject well worthy of a book of its own. Unfortunately this is a book about American foreign policy; the topic of the changing nature of capitalism is too important to our subject to ignore, but too complicated and too rich to treat fully. It is quite possible that a more thorough study of the subject would lead to a somewhat different treatment of the new capitalism than I am giving it here. I am not trying to give a full and theoretically coherent description of anything as complicated as a new (and still emerging) form of social and economic organization; I am just trying to highlight some of the most significant features of a set of changes that are reshaping the choices facing American foreign-policy makers.

Because I have to call it something, and because the obvious terms of Reaganite and Thatcherite capitalism are too dated and one sided to describe a phenomenon that is still growing and changing, I have chosen to call the new capitalism "millennial capitalism." This is partly because the new capitalism is taking shape around the turn of the millennium, and partly because its emergence causes both its supporters and its opponents to indulge in near-apocalyptic hopes and fears. It is also a neutral term; both those who like the new system and those who hate it can call it millenial capitalism without compromise or concession.

Millennial capitalism is not simply a return to the laissez-faire capitalism of an earlier age. In 1900 the federal budget stood at an estimated 3 percent of GDP.* We are not headed back in anything like that direction. The gold standard is not about to return; money will remain a frankly artificial and political measure of value and central banks will continue to intervene in the credit markets. Fiscal stimulus is still very much with us as a policy tool, and the panoply of social insurance programs dating back to the New Deal and beyond in the United States, and back to Bismarck's day in Europe, will be overhauled, trimmed, and reformed, but not abolished.

It is a great misunderstanding to suppose that millennial capitalism is simply a matter of deregulation. Many of the structures of Fordist regulation have been overturned, but new forms are taking their place. In Fordist capitalism, the market was seen as a dangerous force

---

* *Historical Statistics of the United States: Colonial Times to 1970* (White Plains, NY: Kraus International Publications, 1989), 224, 1114.

that had to be harnessed and restricted. Ordinary people needed to be protected from its vagaries.

In millennial capitalism, the role of regulation is to protect the existence and efficiency of markets in order to allow wider access to their benefits. One can argue over the wisdom of proposed reforms like substituting individual retirement accounts for programs like Social Security, and there is much to be said on both sides, but the intent of the changes is to allow individuals more opportunities to accumulate assets and to gain higher returns on their retirement savings. Fordism sought to protect consumers in monopoly industries like electricity or water from the abuse of monopoly power through preventive regulation. Millennialism seeks to achieve the same results by promoting more competition among what had previously been considered natural monopolies. Both types of regulation lend themselves to abuses, and the record of millennial reform has not always been inspiring, but there is a vast difference between the flexible regulatory networks millennial capitalism proposes and the utter absence of regulation that characterized the apogee of Victorian capitalism.

National regulation may be decreasing, but the rise of millennial capitalism is creating new forms of international regulation that simply did not exist in the past. Free-trade agreements are much more than trade agreements; they create new transnational forms of regulation and justice. Foreign investment, industrial subsidies, environmental practices: they all face new kinds of scrutiny from new kinds of institutions.

Millennial capitalism is also driven in part by the demographic shift now taking place in so much of the world. As population growth shrinks and goes into reverse, many of the social and economic policies of the demographic booms no longer make sense. Medical and pension insurance programs in particular are becoming less and less viable in many economies; for these programs to continue to work, the rate of return on savings (both social and individual) must rise. In general, this means that investment decisions need to move from state allocation and subsidy programs to market-driven, yield-sensitive investments. This shift has enormous implications for political and financial systems across the globe and it plays a major role in driving the economic shift.

Another factor that needs to be mentioned is that millennial capitalism is a natural and logical outgrowth of Fordism itself. A Fordist society is a consumer society; liberated from the need to spend every last bit of money on the basic necessities of life, Fordist consumers begin to express themselves through the kinds of cultural products they buy and the resulting social and cultural changes can ultimately no longer be satisfied within the framework of Fordist society.

The empowered consumers of a developed Fordist society increasingly bring a consumers' psychology to social institutions as well. The Baby Boom in the United States, the first generation with no memory of anything but a Fordist society, refused to take existing institutions and limits for granted, reinventing everything from religion to government to social institutions like marriage. The Fordist individual no longer wants to be part of a bloc, nor is he or she prepared to delegate control over political and social decisions to a handful of leaders. The regimentation, discipline and passivity before power that, for example, New York–area householders were expected to exhibit when Robert Moses wanted to put a freeway through their property, disappears as the consumer psychology spreads among voters. The cultural contradictions of capitalism observed by Daniel Bell might be more usefully understood as cultural contradictions in Fordism. The social conditions promoted by Fordist society steadily undermine the cultural, psychological and political foundations of that society.

It is also important to draw a distinction between millennial capitalism as an analytic concept and globalization. Globalization is to some degree a consequence of millennial capitalism and the two phenomena are clearly related, but globalization has been used so widely to describe so many different phenomena that we need a term that focuses more on the structural dimensions of the changes remaking so much of the world. Globalization and millennial capitalism are related, but they are not the same thing.

The shift away from Fordism has much greater implications for world politics and, especially, for America's hegemonic power than we often realize. Globally, the shift from Fordism is deeply unpopular with three audiences, and, unfortunately, they are key audiences for American foreign policy. By and large, governments and the established classes around them *hate* millennial capitalism. In a Fordist world economy, governments were able to steer credit toward selected regions, sectors, and companies. Japan and other Asian countries used this system to build world-class exporting economies. In Germany, France, and much of western Europe, state involvement in the economy not only helped build a planned and stable manufacturing prosperity; it also allowed the creation of the welfare systems that ended a century of social conflict. In Latin America, the system allowed the creation of national industries that established islands of affluence for significant sectors of the population, but also provided governments with instruments of social and political control. Even in Africa, where economic policy of all kinds was mostly a dismal failure, the ability of the state to control and direct economic activity and resources, however poor the results for development, was absolutely necessary for the fragile political and social stability that existed in most countries for at least the first decades of independence.

As the United States moved from Fordism to millennialism, and as both its government policy and, perhaps more importantly, its corporations and investors exerted increasing pressure on the world to move toward millennialism, the nation, in effect, was becoming the enemy of every other state in the world. France, Syria, Brazil, Japan, South Korea, Nigeria, Argentina, and many others are one in resenting and resisting the "neoliberal globalization" that threatens their ability to shape domestic economic and political events. A conflict was growing that Karl Marx would have recognized and accurately interpreted: a conflict between the "cosmopolitan" capital of the global, millennial system and the "national" capital of countries whose elites were desperately protecting their Fordist and statist systems against the new threats.

In the Cold War our military and political power was preserving the independence of these states while our economic system was enriching and empowering them. Now our predominant political and military power threatens to eclipse and marginalize them in the "unipolar world" of which we are so fond, while our economic policy aims systematically to strip them of their power at home. The only surprise here is that so many Americans were surprised at the rise of political opposition to American policy and of anti-American political cooperation on a broad global scale.

If opposition was limited to states and the elites closely aligned to them, this would be a difficult enough foreign policy problem. Unfortunately, the problem goes much further—to the beneficiaries, real or aspiring, of the old Fordist system. When Europeans read in their morning papers that their government wants to raise the retirement age, cut unemployment benefits, increase co-payments for health care, or raise college tuition, many people curse the United States and the neoliberal globalization they feel it is forcing on the world. Politicians are eager to assist them with the cursing; blaming unpopular measures on the insidious "Anglo-Saxon" model of capitalism now spreading throughout the world is a good way to deflect hostility for unpopular measures.

In the developing world the attachment to the subsidies, protected niches, and social legislation of the Fordist era runs even deeper, even though in many countries only a minority of the population may receive substantial benefits. In countries like Egypt, Peru, and Malaysia, governments provide secure and usually not too demanding ways of making a living for a lucky percentage of the population. The "establishment" in these countries is usually closely linked to the government, and fiercely defensive of its own privileged position. When outside economic forces or agencies—currency markets, the International Monetary Fund, the United States—push for unpopular changes, the politically active and educated minority is almost unanimous in its resentment and resistance. Again, when concessions are necessary, politicians blame unscrupulous but irresistible pressure from all-powerful and malign "neoliberals" and "Washington consensus" bureaucrats. The result is a poisonous mix of anti-American sentiment that grew steadily throughout much of the world while Americans congratulated themselves on their irresistible soft power during the lost years.

The situation varies from country to country and region to region, and not all the consequences of the economic shift have been negative. America's willingness to accept large trade deficits has helped to improve relations between the United States and China, for example. On the other hand, in Asian countries that experienced the worst effects of the 1997 financial crisis, a popular suspicion of, and even at times hatred of, the United States as an arrogant, indifferent force has grown steadily.

In most cases it is not American diplomatic pressure (either direct or indirect through the IMF and the World Bank) or even American economic pressure that is responsible for economic change. Fordism is coming to an end because it is no longer the most efficient method to organize capitalist production. The subsidies, costs, and state interference of the old system ultimately create a web of costs, corruption, vested interests, and irrational allocations of resources that can no longer be tolerated. Like water seeking the path of least resistance and its own level, capital seeks the countries, the industries, and the firms in which it can earn the best returns. When it is blocked in one direction, it flows harder and faster in others. Countries that restrict its free search for profit quickly discover that the capital they invest earns a lower rate of return than capital in other parts of the world.

None of this matters much in the contest for public opinion. We now live in a world in which hundreds of millions, if not billions, of people are firmly convinced that the unwelcome and confusing changes roiling their lives bear a "Made in the USA" label.

Xenophobic hatred of "Made in America" globalization is strongest in the Middle East, where half a century of support for Israel had already laid a strong basis for anti American feelings. The Arab world includes some of the leading examples of "failed Fordism." State-led development and education strategies in these countries failed to generate the kind of prosperous, diversified economies one sees in Europe and Asia. Instead, the network of protected industries, civil service positions, and subsidies to politically important constituencies created a kind of pseudo–middle class. In income and aspirations this class is something like the mass middle classes that Fordism creates in more successful economies; unlike those classes, however, the pseudo–middle class is dependent on government jobs or patronage. Even business takes place in a stifling atmosphere of licensing, regulation, corruption, and protection.

Miserable as this system is, and limited as its successes have been, in its heyday it managed the transition from colonialism to independence and saw the construction of such basic elements of industrial life as a power grid and urban infrastructure. Talented young people had far more opportunity than ever before to escape the confines of village life, and a spotty and partial modernization occurred in most Arab countries.

Arab Fordism has been in crisis for some time. As in other countries, the hidden and direct costs of Fordist subsidies climb as years go by. Every old and outmoded subsidy has a constituency fiercely fighting to save it; the costs of industrial protection and isolation proliferate in ways that are hard to measure but easy to see as national firms grow increasingly backward and the goods they offer become increasingly shoddy and costly by world standards. As in many developing countries, the state's economic power has often gone to the head of the political elite. Control over credit allocation and economic activity has been used to cement a political machine so powerful that opposition withers, and sloth and corruption reign largely unchecked.

The population explosion in the Arab world has dramatically worsened these problems. Every year more young people graduate from universities, but stagnant businesses and government bureaucracies can absorb only a fraction of them. The vibrant, successful Fordist societies of North America and western Europe thrived on the demographic growth that ensured an expanding workforce for economies that had largely mastered the secrets of full employment in the regulated national economies of the advanced industrial democracies in the post–World War II world. The Fordism manqué of developing countries, and especially in the Arab world, has been unable to rise to this challenge. An educated proletariat forms of capable people who have no prospects for the economic security they have been educated to expect and demand. Civil engineers, lawyers, doctors, and dentists are economically marginalized and lack the patrons who would land them secure state or state-supported employment. Because most Arab countries now offer very limited political options, these dissatisfied citizens are unable to express their resentment through conventional political channels. This population has been a prime source for the alternative Islamicist establishment: a nonstate alternative source of employment built on frustration and, in part, rage.

Into this cauldron now comes the demand—portrayed as made in America regardless of where it comes from—to dismantle the subsidies, open economies to outside competition, allow foreign investment, and do all the other difficult things millennial capitalism requires. The same United States that everyone knows is in the pocket of the Zionist war criminals, the source of the pornographic and disturbing entertainment and ideas that are corrupting the youth, that makes alliances with corrupt local tyrants and oil sheiks to steal resources that properly belong to the people—this United States is now demanding that the entire country be drawn into a whirlpool of usury and misery.

The gap between the Arab Middle East and the United States is only broadened by the way that the transition from Fordism to millennial capitalism in the United States heightened the aspect of Fordist society that was always difficult for the Middle East to accept: the increased ability of women and homosexuals to flout convention and live in their own way. In American life, but even more dramatically in the representations of American life disseminated through the global media, more and more people were acting in ways that challenged the ability of Muslim society in particular to defend traditional values. The increased access to foreign media throughout the Middle East meant that the image of a newly libertine post-Fordist America was almost impossible for traditionalists and worried parents to keep out of their homes. From a conservative Middle Eastern point of view, the increased military power of the United States, the deeper penetration of its increasingly immoral media, the increased power and presence of its economic model and methods combined to make the American presence in the region all but unendurable to large numbers of people. It will take more than a few TV spots and scholarships to overcome these problems.

SIX

Bush, the Neocons, and the American Revival

Much of the world might like to go back to Fordist political economy and stay there, but the ideas and values of the new form of millennial capitalism are becoming increasingly dominant in the Republican Party and, beyond that, in American life.

It turns out that in many ways the social attitudes and values that millennial capitalism fosters have a lot in common with the traditional Anglo-American individualism that Fordism tended to marginalize and suppress. This historical accident is responsible for some of the strange political labels now found in American discourse. The revolutionary partisans of millennial capitalism who want to take a wrecking ball to the surviving Fordist structures and social programs are called "conservatives." Their opponents, desperately trying to preserve an endangered status quo, are called "liberals."

The promoters of millennial capitalism are not, like the old, anti–New Deal American conservatism, a counterrevolutionary protest against Fordism with at least one foot firmly planted in the anticapitalist (and racist) agrarianism of the Old South. The new movement feels the winds of history at its back; it increasingly attracts young people to its side and feels it is fighting for the future.

American Revivalists, as we can call those who support the shift toward millennial capitalism, are not only
attempting to revive the individualism and other values of pre–New Deal America, they believe that the new
freedoms and policies they support will lead to a revival
of American power (and American values) around the
world.

This is an assertive, self-confident ideology that after a
generation of steady progress no longer feels itself on the
defensive in domestic politics, and which believes that
its domestic victories herald nothing less than the dawn
of a second American century in world affairs. Revivalists believe that the new revolution is not only as necessary as the Fordist revolution once was, they also believe
that, like Fordism, the new political economy can ultimately serve as the platform for a new and progressive
recasting of the American project for world order.

The ambition of the American Revivalists is not simply to add one more voice to the American chorus of
political discussion. Their goal—and they are closer to it
than many realize—is to replace the debate of the last
fifty years with a new debate. They do not simply want to
make the Republican Party the dominant party in American politics, they want to claim the terrain over which
both parties contend.

The Revivalists are as ambitious in foreign policy as
they are in domestic affairs. Historically, American foreign policy has been shaped by debates among economic
nationalists (Hamiltonians), idealistic internationalists
(Wilsonians), isolationists (Jeffersonians), and populist
nationalists (Jacksonians). The American Revivalists aren't
trying to establish a fifth party in American politics to
contend against the other four; they are trying to take
over all of the four older parties and remake them in the
light of American Revival ideas.

One of the clearest signs that the American Revival is
not a reactionary movement is the degree to which much

of its thinking has roots in the Hamiltonian party in American life, historically the group that represents the advanced thinking of the American business elite. In George Washington's administration, Alexander Hamilton put together a coalition of wealthy business and financial leaders who understood the importance of a strong national government for the American economy. Theodore Roosevelt considered himself a Hamiltonian and many of the progressive reformers who midwived the rise of Fordist capitalism in America came out of this school. The popularity of American Revival ideas among Hamiltonians today reflects the degree to which structural changes in the American economy are driving and shaping the new ideologies now contending for power.

Just as Hamiltonians took the lead in fashioning the Fordist consensus—and in translating its ideas into foreign policy—so a new generation of Hamiltonians has played a major role in shaping the new, post-Fordist political economy. In the twentieth century, American business became more institutionalized and institutionally minded than it had been historically. For most of our history, there was an enormous rapidity to the rise and fall of industries and firms, but the years from about 1923 to 1973 saw an unusual degree of stability in American enterprise, except for the turmoil of the Great Depression. For some of that period, a relatively smooth relationship between big business and big labor saw the rents of oligopolies and large monopoly enterprises (like AT&T) shared among key stakeholders. Business by and large accepted and even came to welcome the regulatory climate of the New Deal and subsequent years, believing that the advantages of macroeconomic stability and social peace outweighed the costs of inflexibility and taxation that the new system imposed. The old Rockefeller Republicans and their moderate Democratic colleagues reflected this vision, which was at its strongest in American politics between about 1940 and 1975.

The increasingly dominant Revival Hamiltonians reflect what remains, even after the bursting of the dot-com and technology bubbles, a profoundly changed and reenergized American business landscape. Since the seventies, Wall Street has been moving toward a more and more wholehearted embrace of unfettered competitive capitalism. The pace of business competition has heated up and in many ways the dynamism of American business competition today surpasses the white-hot intensity of nineteenth-century American capitalism: huge industries rise and fall—or move overseas—within a single decade. Flexibility has become more important for America's cutting-edge businesses than macroeconomic stability. The European Union, seen as a slowly growing and rapidly aging "mature" market that perpetually demands an unreasonable price in global trade talks and on such matters as antitrust regulation, is no longer the automatic prime partner for the new Hamiltonians that it was (and still is) for the old. Support for free trade is one of the few points of continuity between old and new Hamiltonians; on this point, they both disagree with the nineteenth-century Hamiltonians who believed that industrial protection was necessary to support the growth of American industry.

A key aspect of the new Hamiltonian approach to foreign policy is the role of the new high-tech military-industrial complex. The revolution in military affairs, with its emphasis on a new military that will rely more on advanced weapons systems including space-based systems, is not only a strategy that proponents hope will increase the American advantage over other military powers, it also, advocates claim, makes the defense budget a powerful engine of economic development: government defense spending will, they argue, stimulate new generations of research and development into cutting-edge technologies. Whether this will work is not clear; classic laissez-faire economists would argue that government intervention will simply divert capital from more productive research and investments into less useful and effective military technologies. Whatever the outcome, the new industrial sectors that will grow up around the military transformation and the civilian spin-offs they will generate will become a major political factor, just as the old aerospace industry supported Cold War hawks like Henry "Scoop" Jackson in Washington State and Ronald Reagan and Richard Nixon in California.

There is one more difference between Fordist and Revival Hamiltonians: confidence. The Fordist-Hamiltonian business establishment of the Cold War era believed that first parts of western Europe and Japan and then parts of the developing world would overtake the United States. It is largely forgotten today, but during the 1950s and 1960s both western Europe and Japan grew much faster than the United States by virtually every performance measure, from productivity growth to unemployment. By the 1970s the first signs of the growth miracle in Asia were becoming apparent and the 1980s were a decade in which it seemed to many observers (including me) as if the period of American economic and technological supremacy had ended. Since then, the tables have turned once more, and the American economy has outdistanced its rivals—and, at least for the moment, the lead looks reasonably durable. As a result, Revival Hamiltonians have more faith than their predecessors that the unique features of Anglo American political economy hold the secret to success, and that if the United States remains true to its own values, it will continue to dominate the cutting edge of global technological innovation and economic dynamism. The structural weaknesses of the European economies (and the demographic decline of European populations) will make them weak competitors; the institutional weaknesses and political problems of

East and South Asia along with Latin America reduce America's need to worry about new challenges from those parts of the world.

While the American Revival is transforming some Hamiltonians, the Wilsonian party in American foreign policy is being born again. Literally. The mainline Protestant denominations that shaped the American Wilsonian tradition of progressive internationalism are losing strength to evangelical and fundamentalist denominations. The Catholic Church, another source of support for institutionalized multilateralism as a basis for American foreign policy, was already in a period of profound crisis and change before the clerical sexual scandals paralyzed its national leadership. And just as a coalition of conservative Christian and Jewish supporters of Israel changed the traditional Republican approach to the Israeli-Palestinian question, the same coalition is developing a new version of the Wilsonian agenda in American international relations.

From the debate over the Treaty of Versailles to the present day, Wilsonian opinion in the United States focused on three ideas: one, that there is a vital linkage between American security and the determined pursuit of American values through foreign policy; two, that rule-based global institutions should play a growing and ultimately decisive role in international life; and three, particularly as mainline Protestantism left its theological zeal behind and as Catholics, Jews, and nonreligious Americans played a growing role in Wilsonian politics, that questions of value should be addressed in primarily secular terms rather than using the Protestant Christian values message of earlier generations.

Revival Wilsonians, whose ranks include the majority of the neoconservative policy intellectuals who have played such an important role in Republican foreign policy debates in recent years, have radically restructured the Wilsonian agenda. They put the first element—the linkage between idealism and security—on steroids, arguing, for example, in the case of the Middle East, that only a much more aggressive pursuit of American ideological values can deal with the security threats we now face. The disdain for Clintonian nation-building so widely heard in the early years of the Bush administration turns out to be a disdain for nation-building in an old Wilsonian context of international institutions and secular values. Just as Revival Hamiltonians are confident in the ability of the American economy to outdistance the competition based on the revival of traditional American values represented by millennial economics, Revival Wilsonians believe that traditional American values are so compelling, so demonstrably superior, and so widely popular that they can sweep and reshape the world.

Revival Wilsonians are conspicuously less confident about the second element of the progressive Wilsonian agenda. The old Wilsonians believed (and believe) that international institutions provide a necessary legitimacy and objectivity for exercises of American power in the service of human rights and international values. Furthermore, while embracing the concept of universal human rights, they reject the idea that one nation, however enlightened, can and should serve as the world's judge, jury, and enforcer. Wilsonians have traditionally belonged to the Party of Heaven, seeking to transcend what they see as a narrow and inherently dangerous and flawed model of American domination for a genuinely consensual, legal, and even militarily supreme international government.

Here the cultural and historical experiences of sectarian Protestants and persecuted Jews have come together to produce a passionate dissent to the old Wilsonian internationalist orthodoxy. The non-mainline American Protestant tradition was built on suspicion and rejection of universal institutions like the Catholic Church, and the rejection of the ideal of a single world state is an important part of the theological worldview of contemporary American evangelicalism. Modern European Jewry watched the "world community" stand aside as millions of Jews perished in the Holocaust; since then Jews have watched the General Assembly, the chief political representative of that "world community," indulge itself in decades of what they see, reasonably, as vicious, one-sided, and at some level anti-Semitic attacks on the Jewish state established as a refuge for the victims of persecution.

As the Psalmist asks, "Why do the nations rage so furiously together? And why do the people imagine a vain thing against the Lord and His Anointed?" Right-wing American Christians have united with many American Jews not only to defend Israel against its enemies but also against what they see as the deeply flawed and even wicked moral basis of most of the world's ruling elites. For Revival Wilsonians, the United States must enforce universal principles and values in the teeth of what is likely to be bitter opposition from the institutions and elites that the old Wilsonians saw as natural and necessary allies.

The alliance of realpolitik with a values-based foreign policy that is one of the hallmarks of neoconservative thought and the new Wilsonianism strikes many observers as an unlikely and unsustainable combination. It is, however, more comprehensible if one understands that, for neoconservatives and Revival Wilsonians generally, American power is itself the *summum bonum* of world politics. The end is so noble—the preservation and enhancement of the only power capable of leading the world in a positive direction—that realist means are fully justified. Once again, a parallel with Israeli experience can be drawn. The Jewish state can be the expression of the ideals of the Jewish people only if it can be the guardian of their physical security; therefore one can advocate an idealistic Zionism while also supporting a realistic foreign policy for the state.

This shift is contributing to the reenergizing of American foreign policy. The general tendency of Wilsonian foreign policy is for an active, interventionist United States. A sense of moral duty drives Wilsonians to seek out monsters that more realist thinkers are generally content to leave unmolested. In the old Wilsonianism, however, this interventionist impulse was somewhat checked by Wilsonian ideas of international law, the morality of nations and a preference for working within international institutions. Revival Wilsonianism is less inhibited. Having made its peace with realpolitik, it can only be dissuaded from activist foreign policy on pragmatic grounds.

Paradoxically, the rise of Wilsonian realpolitik is accompanying a trend among Revival Wilsonians to promote specifically Christian rather than liberal secular humanist values in foreign policy. Returning to Wilsonianism's nineteenth-century roots among missionaries and fervent Protestants, Wilsonian Revivalists are building a strong coalition that binds the Christian right to an assertive, long-term strategy of intervention and, yes, nation-building abroad, even as they embrace a program of strengthening religious values and institutions at home. Partly because of the reinforcements born-again Wilsonians bring to American policy and power in the Middle East, and partly because conservative secularists and Jews can share the fears of the Christian right about the long-term impact of an aggressively secular and pleasure-seeking public culture on the moral fiber and therefore the strength of the American people, many non-Christian conservatives are reasonably comfortable with this dimension of the emerging form of Wilsonian ideology in American life. The cultural hegemony of liberal, Fordist ecumenism is being challenged by a millennial, conservative ecumenism in domestic as well as foreign policy.

This is an ideology whose power can easily be misunderestimated by those who do not share its assumptions. The projection of religious faith and values onto the

arena of foreign policy has tremendous appeal and reso-
nance for tens of millions of Americans. The (literally)
apocalyptic hopes and fears awakened by events in the
Middle East—and the war on terror—reinforce this traditional preoccupation of the American mind at a time
when religious interest seems to be growing not only in
the United States but around most of the world as well.
The question of Africa, where humanitarian disaster on
a vast scale exists side by side with a conflict between
Islam and Christianity over the future religious faith of
this huge and strategic continent, provides an arena where
national interest and religion are mixed in important
ways. The ability of Revival Wilsonians to draw African-
American support for a faith-based approach to Africa
should not be discounted, and will probably not be discounted by Republican political strategists.

With regard to the alliance between evangelical Christians and Orthodox Jews, skeptics note that evangelical
Christians believe that unless Jews receive Christ as their
savior they will burn everlastingly in the flames of Hell.
This belief, added to the millennia of Christian anti-
Semitism, should, they argue, ensure that sooner or later
the Orthodox-evangelical alliance must break.

What they miss, though, is that many evangelical
American Christians today, unlike most of their Christian predecessors throughout history, are willing to leave
the conversion of the Jews to God. The most widely
accepted interpretations of biblical prophecy among
American evangelicals predict mass conversions of Jews
to Christianity in the last days, but predict it as the result
of an unlooked-for miracle of God rather than as the
result of missionary endeavors by Christians. While no
doubt always eager to help individual religious seekers of
Jewish origin find Christ, and while organizations like
Jews for Jesus continue to proselytize among Jews,
today's American evangelical Christians are mostly ready
to leave the religious future of Israel in God's hands while

standing against its enemies in the here and now. With a common concern for the future of Israel and a common opposition to the corrupt false conscience of the "world community" to bind them abroad and a common opposition to the secularization of American culture at home, American evangelicals and Orthodox Jews appear set to write a new and original chapter in the long and troubled story of relations between the faiths. Their alliance could well be deeper and more stable than many observers believe.

Moreover, the deinstitutionalization of the Wilsonian project that the Revival Wilsonians propose is potentially popular with many Americans. Wilsonian human rights and democratic values are much more popular among Americans than Wilsonian institutions. The run-up to the war in Iraq provided a striking illustration of the weakness of American support for international institutions. Throughout the fall of 2002 and the winter of 2003, confident old Wilsonians and their European allies looked at polls saying that large majorities of Americans wanted UN approval for any invasion. This seems to have led the French, among others, to overestimate the price that the Bush administration was prepared to pay in order to get Security Council authorization for an invasion. They did not ask themselves what polling would show if Americans were asked whether France, Russia, and China should jointly or severally possess a right of veto over actions defined by an American president as necessary for his country's self-defense. Once the question was put in that form, American public opinion moved solidly (if perhaps temporarily) behind war with only a coalition of the willing. Unilateralism in the defense of liberty is no vice, as Barry Goldwater might have said.

A principled preference for multilateralism is always a difficult proposition to defend in American politics. Although many critics of Bush's foreign policy have criticized what they see as a failure of the administration to follow a more multilateral approach, one only needs to turn to the liberal wing of the Episcopal Church to see how shallow this principled multilateralism actually is. The decision by the Diocese of New Hampshire to ordain an non-celibate gay man as bishop set off a widespread crisis in the Anglican Communion, with mostly conservative African bishops (representing a majority of Anglican believers in the world) bitterly opposed to what they saw as a unilateral action by American Episcopalians. The Right Reverend Frank Griswold, one of the most vocal critics of Bush's foreign policy, defended the stand of the New Hampshire diocese and the American branch of the church on the grounds that this was a matter of conscience. The Holy Spirit was leading American Episcopalians to embrace lesbians and gays as full members of the Body of Christ. To subject the call of the Spirit to interminable deliberations in international institutions was a violation of conscience and Christian duty. In Episcopalian politics, it is the conservatives—often political backers of the Bush administration—who bemoan liberal unilateralism and call for a multilateral approach. For most Americans, multilateralism is a stick minorities use to attack majority policies they oppose in a high-minded and emotionally satisfying way. Disentangling the Wilsonian impulse from the obligations of principled multilateralism is unlikely to hurt the Revival Wilsonians and will contribute to the ability of neoconservatives and their allies to push American foreign policy in a more activist direction.

Finally, since the neoconservative movement remains at the cutting edge of Revival Wilsonianism, many observers note that there aren't really that many neoconservatives even in the Republican Party, and, especially after neoconservative optimism about the prospects for rapid progress in post-conflict Iraq proved overstated, they anticipate that the neoconservative movement may have passed its apogee of influence in American politics.

Prediction, as they say, is always hazardous, and especially when it involves the future, but I would personally not be too quick to write off Revival Wilsonians.

It is in the nature of American religion that the religious establishment will seek to shape American foreign policy to reflect its values. The rise of conservative, evangelical, Pentecostal, and fundamentalist religious movements, one of the largest and most important cultural developments in the United States over the last generation, has laid the foundation for a new kind of religious establishment. In the recent past, the religious right has felt itself to be standing outside the policy process, especially the foreign policy process. Increasingly, the leaders of the rising religious forces in this country will find themselves on the inside of the process, helping to shape it. To the extent that American foreign policy comes to revolve around a struggle with Middle Eastern fanatics who believe themselves to be fighting a war of religion against the United States, the conservative Protestant religious leadership of the United States will play a major role in articulating the values and ideas for which many Americans will be willing to fight.

The neoconservative movement—relatively small in numbers, northeastern and socialist in original background, disproportionately Jewish by ethnicity—will probably lose some of its relative power as the Revival Wilsonian camp grows and develops. The final form of a developed Revival Wilsonianism may smack more of the Bible Belt than of the borscht, and it may lose some of the intellectual rigor that has always been one of the great strengths of the neoconservative movements. It may look more like a religious movement and less like an intellectual one, but it is likely to be much larger than it now is, and have deeper roots in popular organizations and loyalties than it now does. The Apostle who carries the neoconservative gospel to the gentiles may transform the movement as profoundly as Paul of Tarsus transformed the early "Jesus movement" when he founded the gentile church; but it looks to me as if an emerging and growing Revival Wilsonian movement will be the channel through which neoconservative insights reach millions of people who have never heard of *Commentary*.

Meanwhile Revival Wilsonians face the same basic problem that their unregenerate colleagues have faced in the past. Generally speaking, the American people are not willing to send military forces (and dollars) to all the places and for all the causes Wilsonians support. The Clinton administration faced these limits in Haiti and the Balkans; the Bush administration discovered them in the testing months between the fall of Baghdad and the capture of Saddam Hussein. Wilsonians old and new can make grand speeches about restructuring the Middle East, but a skeptical Congress and public opinion have to be convinced (sometimes over and over) that this is necessary and possible.

The neoconservatives and their born-again colleagues are probably more vulnerable to the temptations of Wilsonian overstretch than the Fordist Wilsonians who have been coping with these limits since the rejection of the Treaty of Versailles. Nevertheless, they are fast learners, and demographics are on their side. The rise in the number of evangelical Protestants, combined with their increasing levels of affluence, political participation, and education, suggest that for the next generation at least we will be witnessing the rise and consolidation of an evangelical establishment that will view America's world role in a different way than the waning and dying mainstream Protestant establishment that once set the Wilsonian agenda. Anyone who thinks that Revival Wilsonianism is a passing or temporary phenomenon in American foreign policy is misreading the signs of the times.

The rise of Hamiltonian and Wilsonian factions influenced by the American Revival ideas helped set the stage for a new era in American foreign policy, but the key to the political change in American society and, therefore, to the changing orientation of American foreign policy is the decline in support for Fordism by the popular American nationalists I called "Jacksonians" in my book *Special Providence*. The decline of social democratic values among the so-called Reagan Democrats of the northern industrial (and ex-industrial) states, and the increasing attraction of classical Anglo-American individualism among the descendants of the late-nineteenth- and early-twentieth-century immigrant communities of the United States, combined with the rise of the modern Republican Party in the ex-Confederate states, were profound changes in American culture the impact of which has yet to be fully felt. Stripped of most of the disfiguring legacy of racism that was once such an integral part of American populist identity, divorced from the naïve agrarianism that made the old American populism so skeptical of markets, the mix of American exceptionalism, anti–big government populism, and defiant individualism that characterized much of rural and small-town America one hundred years ago, and which seemed as doomed as the village blacksmith by the time of the New Deal, had become a major political force in the land by the start of the twenty-first century.

Politically and culturally, the collective, institutional nature of Fordist society had always been its Achilles' heel in the United States. While both forms of activism exist and can be found at all times in American history, compared to much of the world, Americans tend to shun collective social action and solutions to economic problems in favor of individual action. They would rather solve their problems themselves. They would rather get out of the working class than struggle with others to improve working-class conditions. They would rather go to night school and join management than join a union. Sociologists and historians have long struggled to explain why this is so, and the preference is neither universal nor unconditional. Nevertheless, attempts to build parties and trade movements on the basis of economic rather than social and cultural factors have had less success in

American politics than in those of virtually any other advanced industrial democracy.

Fordist society is about classes, masses, and blocs. The era of big business, big labor, and big government was an era of negotiated compromises among large and relatively monolithic blocs. Fordist society is also a highly mediated society with administrators, bureaucrats, and experts given significant autonomy and authority and charged to solve problems like so many angels in the whirlwinds of American life.

Jacksonian America hates that kind of society. It does not trust large institutions or bureaucrats and it believes in keeping "experts" on a short leash. Two generations ago, this suspicion was less important than it is now. The northern and urban immigrants were that much closer to their European origins. They were often comfortable with a world in which the priests and nuns defined right and wrong, the union organized their work and economic life, and the urban political machine handled political questions. In the South, the sheer grinding poverty and added desperation of the Depression made Franklin Roosevelt look like a savior, even if he did stand for big government and even if his wife, Eleanor, had suspiciously liberal views on the race question.

Today the balance of cultural and economic forces in the United States has tilted decisively away from Fordism for many Jacksonians. The descendants of the urban blue-collar immigrant masses live in the suburbs and have learned not to trust politicians, labor leaders, or, especially recently, priests. Southern whites are no longer dependent on the New Deal state for everything from food for their children to electricity in their homes. Doubts about the long-term solvency of Social Security and Medicare have undermined popular confidence in the economic viability of the Fordist model: many Jacksonians have more confidence that big government will collect big taxes than that it will pay out big benefits.

The confluence of traditional American individualism

with the cultural contradictions of Fordism mentioned earlier has created a powerful anti-Fordist dynamic in contemporary American politics. The ethnic ties that were once a building bloc of the social and political institutions of the Democratic New Deal coalition gradually dissolved as Fordist housing policy moved people from ethnic urban neighborhoods into economically rather than ethnically stratified suburbs. The automobiles that Henry Ford wanted the working class to own have created radically different kinds of social and economic interaction. It is no longer the case that the workers in a particular factory tend to live close by the gates; workers now commute across and around vast urban agglomerations. It is rare for Americans to have neighbors who are also colleagues at work; it is rare for members of the same PTA to find themselves standing at the same water cooler in the same office. Increasingly, each American lives in a world that is unique; one's spouse scarcely knows one's coworkers; one's co-religionists play little role in the recreational activities of one's children with little overlap, say, between the T-ball league and the Sunday School. In this environment the kinds of class based political alliances that flourished under and helped build Fordism tend to wither away, and the politics that replaces them tends to highlight what millennial Americans increasingly feel is their true commonality: individualism. Race, gender, and southern regional identity have managed to withstand the full force of the millennial dissolution of traditional forms of political association, but not in ways that, so far, have been able to stop the continuing American political drift away from Fordist values and institutions.

The forest cover of the eastern United States offers a way to grasp the relationship between Fordist and millennial America. When fires clear an area of this forest, coniferous trees like pines are usually the first to flourish. They grow faster than their deciduous rivals, and pine forests quickly rise on the burned over ground. But the pines have a problem: young pines cannot grow in the shade of mature trees—but young hardwoods can. Ultimately, the burned area will revert to what is known as a climax forest: deciduous hardwood trees like maples and oaks.

The Baby Boom grew in the shadow of the mature Fordist forest of fifties America—but Fordist society is not reproducing. Little Fordists don't grow in the shade of a mature Fordist system—and the shade of the Boomers is even less hospitable to the growth of new Fordists among Gen X and Gen Y.

At the same time, a popular revolt against the Fordist mandarinate of experts and officials is gathering steam. A generation of stagnant or declining wages for blue-collar workers and the disintegration of the manufacturing economy have bred an enormous resentment against "the system." To the great frustration of leftists and trade unionists who would have expected—and in many cases are still expecting—a tremendous upsurge of labor protest, a surprisingly large proportion of Jacksonian anger has been expressed against Fordist bureaucracies and social programs. While there have been and still are bitter strikes, successful unionization drives, and deep opposition to free-trade agreements seen as shipping American jobs overseas, lower-middle-class white males have generally moved to the right.

The enemy of Jacksonian America has been largely defined as an arrogant "clerisy" of administrative and cultural elites. Marx would have called this clerisy part of the petite bourgeoisie and he would have been right. Millennial capitalism has much less need of this intermediary class, and one of the main themes in American politics, as well as in American foreign policy, is the class war now raging as the swollen petite bourgeoisie of Fordist society comes under attack from aggressive capitalists, seeking to eliminate its regulatory and intermediary power. Resentful workers also fight against the petite bourgeoisie with its airs of superior moral and intellectual standing. This resentment is a testimony both to deep class-based dislike of the professional and administrative elites (university professors, experts of all kinds, think-tank fellows, lawyers) that Fordism has entrenched and enriched, and to a declining belief in the efficacy of Fordist economic solutions.

What this has led to is a situation in which a Jacksonian revolt against elites is running in harmony with the structural needs of the economy. Disintermediation is the hallmark of the new American economy: reducing costs and raising productivity by eliminating middlemen and middle management. Information technology and the Internet are reducing the need for middlemen like stockbrokers, bank clerks, and travel agents. Markups for middlemen like real estate and mortgage brokers are coming under increasing pressure as consumers use the power of information technology to increase their choices. At the same time, technology helps corporations increase their productivity and thin the ranks of middle management.

We are probably seeing the beginnings of the breakup of the learned guilds—the doctors, lawyers, and tenured university professors who monopolized the production and distribution of knowledge and certain high-end services in the old economy. Consumers can write their wills using cheap software or on the Internet; the fee-for-service model of health-care delivery is under attack on all fronts. As the economic pressures on higher education grow, the tenure system is coming under increasing pressure.

Angels right and left are being chucked out of their whirlwinds. Bureaucrats and experts of all kinds are losing immunity and authority. Popular suspicion of institutions and experts, on the one hand, and the pressure from the business world for radical cost cuts, productivity enhancements, and greater flexibility, on the other, are combining to erode the key structures and practices of a Fordist society.

What has been consistently moving to the fore in American politics is a classic "both ends against the middle" coalition of big enterprises hungry for flexibility and freedom from Fordist constraints and a populist uprising that perceives the administrative middle classes as oppressive and unrepresentative. This is a modern variation on Andrew Jackson's original coalition of outraged populists plus business interests eager to escape the constraints and disciplines of the Bank of the United States and an environment perceived as favoring small elites. The educated classes almost unanimously (though Nathaniel Hawthorne dissented) raised their hands in horror and prophesied everything from massive deficits to economic collapse to a French-style reign of terror. All of these save the last happened, but the growing American economy demanded that the bonds of the old elite be broken, and they were.

Probably much of the background noise of the next generation will be the keen and eloquent wailing of the educated classes in the United States as middle management shrinks before the forces of automation, as the learned guilds are shattered and broken, as the tenured civil service shrinks, and as white-collar jobs are outsourced to developing countries. Those who peacefully contemplated the loss of manufacturing jobs to low-wage competition and automation and who quietly reaped the benefits and composed hymns to the glories of free trade as a generation of blue-collar Americans suffered their greatest shocks since the Great Depression may now find popular sympathy somewhat lacking as the proletarianization of the professions accelerates.

It is likely that party politics will continue to be shaped by the struggle between the Fordist and millennial economies, and both sides will claim significant political victories in the years ahead. Economic necessity will generate continuing pressure to rationalize government, restructure the health-care delivery system, reduce transaction costs and economic friction in the legal profession, as well as cut costs in white-collar work. On the other hand, such a large number of people will have their livelihoods threatened by these changes that political resistance is guaranteed to be sharp and, more than occasionally, effective.

It is also likely that the American party system will rarely give voters a clear choice between two parties—one purely millennial, one purely Fordist. The New Democrats who came to power under President Clinton were in many ways more attuned to the millennial transition than many of the Republicans they defeated. The George W. Bush administration has been more protectionist than President Clinton ever was; its links with the oil industry and its support of massive subsidy increases for such non-cutting edge industries as American agribusiness hardly represent a radical break with American political economy of the mid-twentieth century. The country is likely to move deeper into millennial capitalism as the balance of power within each of the two parties gradually shifts in that direction, following the changing economic and demographic power of important interest groups. At its peak in 1970, manufacturing accounted for 25 percent of the labor force. By 2003, that percentage had fallen to 12.* The New Economy will continue to gain strength; the Old Economy will continue to shrink by comparison. Increasingly, politics will reflect the interests of the rising regions and sectors of the country.

In any case, American Revival ideology and the millennial economic model have been gathering strength in American politics for more than a generation. In domestic politics, they have essentially been dominant forces since Ronald Reagan's election in 1980. Democrats have

* *Economic Report of the President* (Washington, D.C.: Government Printing Office, 2003), 318–319, 330–331.

had to shift steadily toward American Revival positions on virtually every domestic issue, promising a kinder and gentler version of the Revival and supporting Fordist institutions and employment patterns by sleight of hand rather than frankly and openly advocating a return to the old Fordist system.

In foreign policy, the story has been different. Ronald Reagan inaugurated an antiestablishment, American Revival foreign policy, but it was hastily abandoned as the first President Bush moved back toward what were still the mainstream, consensus positions in foreign policy. In the Clinton years, international economic policy moved away from Fordism, as the "Washington consensus" sought to replace the old economic orthodoxies of the Fordist period with "neoliberal" or post-Fordist ideas. In politics and security policy, however, the Clinton administration was staunchly Fordist. The notes of harmonic convergence were still sounding in the Balkans and on the Security Council.

The second President Bush made a much more determined and systematic attempt to place American foreign policy squarely on the basis of American Revival ideas. A mix of incredulity, outrage, shock, anger, and despair is running through the foreign policy establishment as many of its most cherished ideas and institutions are impatiently brushed aside by brusque Jacksonians and Revival Wilsonians. At times it has seemed as if Hell, Heaven, and the petite bourgeoisie of all the world are united in hate and execration for the new direction in American foreign policy. In the vision of the diplomatic establishment in the United States and abroad, the Neanderthals have escaped from their cages and the abomination of desolation has been set up in the holy of holies.

That is much too simple a view. However, an American society increasingly reshaping itself along millennial lines was likely to find increasing problems as it conducted foreign policy in a world in which millennial capitalism was deeply unpopular. Even the increase in American economic and military strength which accompanied the rise of millennial capitalism would cause foreign policy headaches—and all these problems were exacerbated by the shocks that roiled the international system as the United States responded to the attacks of September 11.

PART THREE

Revival in Action

SEVEN

The Foreign Policy of the Bush Administration

It is sometimes easy to forget that despite all the upheaval and turmoil, in many ways the Bush administration has worked within the traditional concerns of American grand strategy: preventing hostile hegemonic powers from establishing themselves in Europe, Asia, and the Middle East; protecting the freedom of the seas and skies; and especially securing the safe and free passage of oil to the world's markets. These remained the cornerstones of the administration's security policy. Maintaining American sticky power as well—keeping the global economic system healthy and open—remained a guiding star of American policy under George W. Bush as it had been for decades. And while many charged that the administration had neglected the concept of soft power, it is a long time since anyone in Washington spoke so powerfully and so confidently about the transformative power of American values as did the neoconservative, Revival Wilsonians who declared that it was their intention to bring pro-American democracy to the Middle East.

"Traditional," however, is not the word that history will use to describe the foreign policy of George W. Bush. And as we review the most striking features of his record, it will be clear that the revolutionary ideology of the

American Revival has been a major influence on his approach to events.

Historians are likely to agree that nothing in the record of the Bush administration is as significant as its decision to describe the struggle that began on September 11 as a—or rather, the—"war on terror," and nothing in its prosecution of that war to date is as significant as its decision to make the invasion of Iraq the centerpiece of its international strategy after smashing Al-Qaeda's bases and sanctuaries in Afghanistan and driving its leaders along with its Taliban protectors and allies into the mountains and caves of that remote and desolate part of the world.

Unlike the decision to retaliate against Afghanistan, both the definition of the problem as a war and the decision to fight it in Baghdad were bitterly controversial choices in the United States and abroad.

"The war on terror" is a catchy phrase, but a clumsy and misleading one, too. In fact, the United States is not fighting a generic war on generic terror; our concern is with what Robert Art calls "grand terror"—terrorism like the attacks on the World Trade Center and Pentagon that create devastation and economic dislocation on a scale approximating that of a war. Currently, the only organizations in the world with both the will and the means to attack the United States on that scale are radical terror groups based in the Islamic world. It is this kind of terror by these people that we are fighting.

Most American allies in Europe and a large section of the domestic foreign policy establishment would have greatly preferred a more "nuanced" and "sophisticated" view of the nature of the challenge rather than simply calling it a war on terror. As former French foreign minister Hubert Védrine said, "We are threatened today by a new simplism which consists in reducing everything to the war on terrorism."* They would have preferred to cope with terrorism as a police and political matter, and saw the problem with Al-Qaeda as a more dangerous but otherwise not dissimilar problem than those posed, say, by the Basque terrorists in Spain or the IRA in Northern Ireland.

It is possible that a President Gore would have tried this approach. If so, he would have faced intense fury and rage from Jacksonian America and Republicans in Congress. Given the power of Jacksonians in the Republican base, it was impossible for George W. Bush to have taken this approach, and there is no evidence that he wished to.

The war on terror is not our first metaphorical war. The Cold War was a metaphor for an international competition that never turned into an armed confrontation between the United States and the Soviet Union. The metaphor has its merits. The Al-Qaeda attacks were more than a hideous act of terrorism. They challenged core elements of American grand strategy in ways that Basque and IRA terrorism never challenged basic elements of British and Spanish security. Besides endangering the security of Americans in their own hemisphere and nation, the Al-Qaeda attacks pose a direct threat to the ever-closer economic ties the United States seeks to build in the world. The symbolic choice of target, the World Trade Center, indicated a sophisticated mind at work, and the tactic of mass terror was well chosen. The attacks significantly exacerbated a damaging recession, and the potential that terrorists would smuggle weapons of mass destruction into New York or other major cities threatened the rapid flow of goods and people on which the American trading system depends. The stated goal of Al-Qaeda's leaders, to build a fundamentalist Islamic

* "Peremptory Tendencies: France Fires a Warning Shot at the US," *The Guardian* (London), February 7, 2002.

caliphate in Saudi Arabia that can unite Muslims into a common struggle against the West, using the oil wealth of the region as a key weapon, is a direct threat to the American presence in a region that every president since Franklin D. Roosevelt has seen as vital to the national interest. While many of the measures that will be taken against Al-Qaeda and its allies will look more like police work (or, at most, covert action by intelligence agencies and Special Forces) than conventional war, the scale of the violence the terrorists are ready to use and the total nature of their demands are more like the actions of a hostile great power than like those of an ethnic resistance movement.

The administration also intended to make the war on terror, which almost certainly will not be concluded rapidly, the replacement for the Cold War as the central organizing idea around which American foreign (and much domestic) policy will be structured for the foreseeable future. Military and intelligence budgets will balloon; the fiscal straitjacket that Ronald Reagan invented to constrain Democratic spending on Fordist social programs will reappear on perhaps a larger scale than before. Although the fortunes of war hold many surprises, it appears likely that war will unite Republicans around a Republican commander in chief, and hard-core conservatives will overlook neglect of some of their less popular domestic agenda items for the sake of supporting a president vigorously prosecuting wars against Christianity-loathing mass murderers. Democrats, on the other hand, might have a hard time uniting behind the kind of moderate pro-war candidates who could seriously contest national elections in a wartime atmosphere. The Cold War saw the end of the Democratic era in American politics that followed Franklin Roosevelt's election in 1932; could a war on terror similarly benefit the American Revival Republicans of today?

When Jacksonian America believes the United States has been attacked and is therefore fighting a necessary war of self-defense, presidents gain enormous authority and have a much easier time getting the resources—foreign aid as well as big military budgets—for a vigorous foreign policy on many fronts. In the Clinton years, the belief by much of the country that we faced no serious dangers overseas led to a steady erosion of both foreign aid and a willingness to defer to the president.

For the Bush administration, declaring war on terror was not only the politically popular course for the short term, it was the choice that allowed the administration to proceed with its projected restructuring of American foreign policy, while at the same time escaping resource constraints that otherwise loomed with the return of large deficits to Washington. It would also allow the changes of alliance priorities and approaches to the United Nations that would take place as the administration moved toward the second, Iraqi phase of its war.

None of this is to suggest that this was a cynical choice, any more than I would suggest that the critics were cynical in wanting to frame the threat as a police problem. Politics, strategic analysis, and personal conviction came together to ensure that for the Bush administration, the attacks of September 11 were the opening salvo in a long, unpredictable war. As Bush told the nation in his address to a Joint Session of Congress on September 20, 2001, "I will not forget this wound to our country or those who inflicted it. I will not yield; I will not rest; I will not relent in waging this struggle for freedom and security for the American people."* There is no doubt that since the destruction of the World Trade Center President Bush has seen himself and the nation he leads in a fight for survival against an utterly unscrupulous, utterly fanatical enemy who would like nothing more than to destroy the United States, its allies, and everything it stands for.

* The White House, *Weekly Compilation of Presidential Documents* (Washington, D.C.: Government Printing Office, September 24, 2001).

. . .

Once war was declared, the administration worked to highlight the differences between its policies and those of previous administrations. In his 2002 State of the Union speech, President Bush introduced the concept of an "axis of evil" of rogue states developing weapons of mass destruction and maintaining links with terrorist groups. Longtime tensions between the United States and Iraq, Iran, and North Korea would now be drawn into the maelstrom of the terror war.

Again, large numbers of critics in the United States and abroad denounced what they saw as a misleading and exaggerated metaphor that, they charged, made the real but limited task of tracking down terrorists harder and more complex than it needed to be. The reaction of the Bush administration was to enshrine the axis of evil states as potential targets for "pre-emptive war" in the document the *National Security Strategy of the United States of America* (NSSD) that it issued in September 2002. Governments that are run by dictators, have links with terrorists, and seek to develop weapons of mass destruction may be the objects of preemptive attacks by the United States. As the president told cadets at West Point on June 1, 2002, "if we wait for threats to fully materialize, we will have waited too long."*

The concept was less new than the language was dramatic. Threats of preemptive war were nothing new in American diplomacy; President Kennedy used the threat of just such an attack to force Nikita Khrushchev to remove nuclear weapons from Cuba. The United States is not alone in the use of preemptive attacks; Britain's attack on the French fleet in the summer of 1940 was intended to preempt any attempt by Germany to seize those assets for itself. Within a year of the publication of

* The White House, *Weekly Compilation of Presidential Documents* (Washington, D.C.: Government Printing Office, June 10, 2002).

the NSSD, the European Union was moving toward a declaration of the circumstances under which it, too, would wage preemptive war against countries attempting to develop weapons of mass destruction.

What was striking about this and other moments in Bush diplomacy was that the administration made no serious effort to calm the anxiety its rhetoric raised. On the contrary, the administration systematically worked to heighten international tensions around its new policies. While critics saw this as part of a pattern of irresponsible crisis mongering, there is little doubt that the administration believed that it was more important to frighten and deter potential enemies than to reassure friends. If the good guys had to be scared in order to make sure the bad guys knew you were serious, so be it. This approach not only reflected the Jacksonian element in the administration, it was also a message to Jacksonian opinion in the United States that the Bush administration considered defense of the American homeland its primary interest and duty, and that nothing, not even relations with allies, would be allowed to compromise this mission.

The next and equally fateful choice of the Bush administration was to invade Iraq and replace the regime of Saddam Hussein. This was largely presented as a timely and essential measure to prevent the regime from adding to its presumed weapons stockpiles and, potentially, transferring these weapons to such groups as Al Qaeda for use against the United States. Once again, there seems little reason to doubt that President Bush and British prime minister Tony Blair sincerely believed that substantial weapons stockpiles would be found following an occupation of Iraq. Saddam had spent more than a decade resisting inspections and enduring sanctions; if the weapons programs were really dismantled and the material disbanded or destroyed, Saddam could have avoided an invasion by cooperating fully with UN inspectors. His repeated refusals to cooperate created a natural and, under the circumstances, actionable presumption that he was in fact developing such weapons. Although there were, as always, discrepancies and gaps in the intelligence information, and although political considerations were clearly leading some policy figures to push for results that, as Dean Acheson would have put it, were "clearer than truth," the preponderance of evidence available from American and British intelligence also pointed to continuing WMD programs in Iraq. It is worth noting that French and German intelligence sources also pointed to the existence of ongoing WMD programs under Saddam.

Pinning the case for war so extensively on the danger presented by Iraqi weapons of mass destruction gave hostages to fortune that the administration (and, much more, Prime Minister Blair) would come to regret during the summer and fall of 2003. Yet the case for invading Iraq was much stronger than fear of WMD, and it was obvious that these considerations were driving U.S. policy on Iraq as much as, or more than, WMD concerns.

Within the Bush administration, there seem to have been three separate lines of argument, related more or less closely to each of the three major ideological trends within it. From a Jacksonian standpoint, the issue was clear-cut though not always discussed in these terms. A sense of clear and present danger from the possibility that Saddam would share his WMD with Al-Qaeda or other terror groups was the stated, rational argument. Another powerful, though less frequently stated, argument held that the United States needed to make a powerful statement to its enemies in the Middle East. Osama Bin Laden appeared to believe that if the United States was attacked and bloodied, it would retreat from the Middle East. He and his followers needed to learn that, if attacked, the United States would not only retaliate, it would advance. Radical Middle Easterners, whether secular Ba'athists or fanatical Islamicists, would have to learn that attacks on America brought overwhelming defeat and deeper humiliation. This was a war, and the enemy had to learn who was the strongest and, if it came to that, the most ruthless. From this standpoint the invasion of Iraq was in the nature of a warning shot: a warning that future attacks on the United States will be followed by even more overwhelming responses.

The neoconservative, Revival Wilsonian approach to the war shared some of this sense of military political realism, but added arguments that had less Jacksonian appeal. The neoconservatives saw the occupation of Iraq as the first stage in the reconstruction of the entire region. In this analysis, it was a war to make the world safe for democracy. Just as Germany and Japan (and Italy, for that matter) made the shift to Western democracy under American tutelage after 1945, Iraq would become the Arab world's first democratic state. As other states saw Iraq's progress, Islamicism and radical Pan-Arab nationalism would lose their allure—economic progress and democratic freedom are contagious. America's military presence in the region and the political consequences of the easy victory over Iraqi forces would have a sobering effect on regimes in Syria, Iran, and the Gulf.

There was also a humanitarian dimension to the neoconservative approach to the war. Saddam's regime was one of the most dreadful in the world, far worse than the very unattractive Ba'ath regime that preceded him and far below even the very modest standards of most modern dictatorships for murder, thuggery, and abuse of the citizenry. Ending this regime would be a good deed; replacing it with a good government would be even better. In this view, the postwar reconstruction of the country would be at least as important as the military campaign to overthrow the old government. The occupation of Iraq was to be the first step in a profoundly deepened American engagement with the Middle East.

A final view with roots in American policy traditions

of power politics and moderate realism was less concerned with the future of Iraq than with ending what was an increasingly expensive strategy of containment. Many critics of the war with Iraq argued that war was unnecessary; containment was working and Saddam was "in his box." Advocates of a strategic war with Iraq argued the contrary case: containment was gradually poisoning and destabilizing the region.

The chief problem was in Saudi Arabia. Saddam's failure to abide by the terms of the 1991 cease-fire agreement meant that American forces needed to be stationed in Saudi Arabia on a permanent basis. That decision so alienated Osama Bin Laden that he broke with the Saudi government and began to organize what would lead to the attacks of September 11. Moreover, the permanent presence of foreign troops so delegitimated the Saudi regime in the eyes of pious (and fanatical) religious opinion that the regime was constantly on the defensive, trying to reestablish its radical Muslim bona fides by pandering to the demands of radical Islamists. It turned a blind eye to Osama's supporters in the kingdom, stepped up support for the most radical and intolerant clerics in the domestic establishment, and ostentatiously continued its support for the worldwide dissemination of the most intolerant and narrow forms of Islamic preaching. All these concessions did not, however, stop the rot in the Saudi kingdom. A visible crisis of legitimacy was growing, and a constant stream of talented Saudi youth were hearkening to voices from the Bin Ladenist wing of radical Islam. Meanwhile, the Saudi government was in no position to take the leadership in the Arab-Israeli peace process.

In these circumstances, American pressure on Saudi Arabia was likely to be counterproductive. If the regime were seen to bow to American pressure, it would lose more legitimacy and strengthen the radicals who hoped to replace it.

There were other problems with containment. The sanctions placed on Iraq after its failures to comply with the original cease-fire agreement and additional UN demands and resolutions were eroding as a result of evasion on the ground and a lack of political will to make them work at the United Nations. Meanwhile, civilian suffering under them was intense, leading to waves of "hate America" propaganda through the region along the lines of accusing Americans of murdering Iraqi children as a deliberate instrument of policy. Taking Iraqi oil off world markets also aided price hawks in the Organization of Petroleum Exporting Countries (OPEC) and heightened the world's dependence on the increasingly rickety Saudi regime. In the meantime, containment left Saddam in control of the political temperature of the Middle East; by firing on British or American planes or otherwise threatening to escape from his box he could plunge the region and the United States into crisis at will.

Containment was a political and humanitarian disaster; ending it with retreat, withdrawal, and the abandonment of sanctions after September 11 was unthinkable. If one can't stay where one is, and one can't go back, the only alternative is to move forward—in this case, toward regime change.

From a strategic point of view, replacing Saddam's Sunni-based minority regime, ideologically committed as it was to Sunni Pan-Arabism, with a new government based in the Shi'a majority and containing protections for the Kurds would be a strategic success even if the new government did not live up to the democratic hopes of the Wilsonians. Modern Iraq had always been run by its Sunni minority, and Pan-Arabism (of necessity, anti-Zionist, anti-Western, and anti-American) was an integral part of the identity of the minority state. Taking Iraq's political weight out of the radical Sunni Arab camp would make a permanent and probably beneficial change in the political geometry of the Middle East, giving better political representation to the cultural, political, and religious diversity that is in fact part of the region's history and identity.

These were the three views of the need for war with Iraq, and while there was some overlap among them and their supporters, they are clear and distinct. It is likely that it took the combined influence of all three lines of argument (and the political constituencies behind them) to set the administration on such a determined course. It was a rich case, but the administration's public case for the war was surprisingly thin. Integrating and harmonizing these complementary and sometimes contrasting approaches to the Iraq problem could have led to greater international support and more durable domestic support for the policy chosen, but this is one of the tasks that, at least so far, the Bush administration has been unable to master.

CIAO EUROPA

After the war itself, the most striking element in the foreign policy of the Bush administration has been its willingness to part company with France and Germany over basic strategic matters. This is more than a quarrel over Iraq; this is a historic change, for the first time in American history, to a non-Eurocentric foreign policy for the United States. In the Bush administration, the strategic focus of the United States moved to the Middle East and Europe fell to third place (behind East Asia) in American concerns.

Traditionally, American grand strategy has viewed Europe as both America's greatest opportunity and America's greatest problem. Europe's dominant position in the international economy, its significance to the United States as the overwhelmingly most important source of immigrants (with all the loyalties that resulted), and its strategic significance as the center of world politics from World

War I through the Cold War all kept American attention fixed on Europe. Today, even as the ties of immigration weaken sentimental ties and Europe has receded as a source of new immigrants, Europe offers America less opportunity and represents less threat than other parts of the world. While Europe remains rich, it is a mature, slow-growing market. Few major barriers to free U.S.-European trade remain, and where they do, it is unlikely that militant and vigilant EU trade negotiators will offer the United States many significant advantages. It seems unlikely that European politics will once again lead to global problems for America. And while Europe can offer both political and military assistance for American policy outside the NATO area, such help is likely to be limited by differences in the interests and priorities of the Europeans compared to the Americans, by the divisions among the Europeans themselves, and by Europe's failure to build significant military power.

European politics make it difficult for the continent to mobilize those resources it has. A France dedicated to limiting American power and a Germany holding the exercise of that power to extraordinarily high-minded standards will, between them, ensure that in many cases Europe is unlikely to provide even the help that it can.

More than that, the Franco-German alliance will have great difficulty identifying any positive foreign policy interests beyond containing the United States and consolidating a Franco-German hegemony in Europe. Germany wants the old games of power politics and national rivalries to end; it has been burned too badly, and both inflicted and suffered too much pain to want to venture down that ominous path again. The French elite, however, like an old and fading roué, just wants to get back in the game. It is addicted to the thrill of the game and it has lost sight of something that both Germans and Americans know: old-fashioned power politics in an era of weapons of mass destruction is a sure road to ruin. Absent a stark and immediate threat to their own security, opposition to American foreign policy is about the only global issue on which this odd couple can agree and, as the Bush administration made plain during the war, any attempt to force the Franco-German consensus on the rest of Europe will draw an immediate response from the United States. The Monroe Doctrine, it turns out, has been extended to Europe, and the French and the Germans will not be allowed to reduce Poland and other dissenting countries to the status of impotent political colonies whose role, as Jacques Chirac so felicitously phrased it, is to "remain silent."

In retrospect, the Clinton years, when the Balkans were the most important focus of administration thinking, seem very far away. For the Bush administration, and almost certainly for its successors of either party, Kurdistan matters more to the United States than Kosovo, and Mesopotamia means more to us than Macedonia. And in American thinking, after the Middle East will not come Europe, but East Asia.

Many Europeans and U.S.-based Bush critics blame the administration for the deterioration in relations that has taken place. To some degree, this is obviously and inescapably true. Before September 11 the Bush administration seemed to take a perverse joy in trampling on European sensitivities. It not only declared the Kyoto Protocol, the Comprehensive Test Ban Treaty, the Landmine Treaty, the U.S.-Soviet Strategic Arms Limitation Treaty, the Protocol on Biological Weapons, and the International Criminal Court dead as far as the United States was concerned, but it also telegraphed its intention to shift American diplomatic interest to relations among "great powers" such as China, Russia, India, and Japan.

Underlying these problems was a radical difference in the way the Bush administration and the Europeans saw Europe's place in the world. After a decade in which the European Union established a common currency, strengthened its core institutions, and negotiated a historic expansion from fifteen to twenty-five members, Europeans felt that they were part of a rising power. Europe might not be a military power like the United States, but it saw itself as an economic superpower, able to hold its own at the World Trade Organization against the United States. Moreover, it had extensive interests in the developing world, where its investments, political contacts, and security and political concerns entitled it, Europeans felt, to a real say in the evolution of global politics.

Also fueling this sense of self-confidence and willingness to take on the United States, was the new feeling of security that came with the end of the Soviet threat. Europe no longer depended on American military power; European leaders were therefore willing to pursue their quarrels and disagreements with the United States much more aggressively than in the past. When NATO was no longer vital to their security, Europeans were willing to take a much harder line with the United States over the Kyoto Protocol.

This European feeling of empowerment and momentum came up hard against the Bush administration's conviction that Europe now mattered less than ever to the United States. From the Bush administration's standpoint, European demands to exercise a veto over American foreign policy (through, for example, the ability of France to veto resolutions authorizing force at the United Nations) were absurd. From the standpoint of Europeans, especially Germans, who were viscerally committed to the establishment of a rule of law in international relations superior to the will of any one country, the Bush decision to proceed with the attack on Iraq without a second Security Council resolution authorizing force was a clear and very unwelcome announcement that the United States did not share their view of the rule of law. More cynical Europeans, of whom there are many, saw the issue in different terms. For them, American power had grown so great that it was becoming a threat to the independence and dignity of the European powers, especially, perhaps, of France.

The French accepted that Al-Qaeda was a threat to all the Western powers and worked with the United States against it, but they had a very different view of regimes like those of Iraq and Iran. From a French perspective, the development of nuclear weapons by countries like Iraq and Iran, though unwelcome, is not as deadly a threat as it is for the United States. For the United States, nuclear proliferation in the Gulf threatens its ability to intervene in a region absolutely vital to its global designs. Europeans can be somewhat more philosophical. The region is, in any case, out of their hands, though they feel confident that the Iraqis and Iranians, nuclear or not, would want to sell oil to Europe. They are also, perhaps, not as worried about a new oil blockade against countries siding with Israel in some future confrontation in the region. It would, after all, be relatively easy for the European states to tilt toward the Arabs enough to avoid a boycott in such an eventuality.

In any case, one might shrug, most realistic foreign policy observers in the United States and elsewhere have thought for many years that wider proliferation was only a matter of time. Why attract Arab enmity by fighting the inevitable?

Probably from this point of view the ideal outcome would be for the United States to succeed in Iraq, but painfully, expensively, and by the skin of its teeth. Europe could stand aside and, with an eye to Arab opinion, deplore the exercise. At the end of the day, the United States would be exhausted, chastened, and much less willing to act without European support in the future.

These considerations made it reasonably likely that Europe—or at least the Franco-German bloc at the heart of the European Union—would stand aside from American policy toward Iraq and, clearly, the Bush administration was unable to bring about a change in this attitude.

The implications for U.S.-European relations in the future are large. If the United States and Europe do not have a joint policy (with whatever differences of emphasis there may be) in the Middle East, then they have little use for each other in international politics. Europe's role in Asia is small; if the United States has trouble with China over Taiwan or with North Korea over its nuclear program, Europe's attitude in the crisis would be essentially irrelevant. With Russia unlikely to pose a serious threat to the rest of Europe in the foreseeable future, there is no defensive agenda in Europe itself to bind the old allies together. If this proves to be the case, and at least some European countries continue to seek to frustrate American policy, it is likely that U.S. policy will shift from promoting the continuing integration of the European Union to ensuring the continuing independence of its member states. As a troublemaker in Europe, building coalitions to frustrate Franco-German plans, and taking advantage of Europe's disagreements and fissures, the United States would enjoy considerable assets.

EIGHT

Where Bush Is Right

It may take historians a long time to reach anything like a consensus over the foreign policy of the Bush administration. But it is already possible to see the basic strengths and weaknesses of the Bush approach.

At the level of basic strategic direction, the Bush administration has, it seems to me, mostly made the right and inevitable choices. The era of Fordist economics and a foreign policy based on harmonic convergence with Europe is, perhaps unfortunately, over. And it has ended for the same reason that it began—the internal necessities and logic of the capitalist economic system that is both the basis of American power and the lodestone of American society. The ideas and values of the American Revival are ingrained in our society, and they continue to gain strength from decade to decade and election to election. This does not mean that the Republicans will have an electoral monopoly going into the future, but it does mean that the task before American society is the continuing deconstruction of the New Deal and its replacement by a new set of institutions and policies that, hopefully, accomplish many of the same goals but use means that reflect the possibilities and requirements of millennial capital rather than the political economy of an earlier time.

Foreign policy must also be much more Jacksonian now. Liberal internationalists, intellectuals, and the "mature" and "sophisticated" ornaments of American petit bourgeois society see the Jacksonian tendencies of the American people as regrettable remnants of a barbarous past that should be suppressed. They would like a foreign policy that ignores those instincts. But that won't work now partly because the American people feel directly threatened and will insist that the country follow a foreign policy that conforms to their intuitive beliefs about how the world works. It also won't work because foreign policy is going to be expensive and demanding; whether one looks at military budgets or foreign aid, Congress is going to have to spend a lot more money on foreign policy than many expected after the end of the Cold War. We are also likely to see American troops stationed abroad and in harm's way. Under these circumstances, foreign policy can't be conducted over the heads or against the basic instincts of the American people. Andrew Jackson won't have the only place at the foreign policy table, and he may not always sit at its head, but he can't be ignored.

If there are more serious attacks on American interests or on American soil, the concern and pressure from Jacksonian America will grow dramatically, and any president of the United States needs to be prepared against this eventuality. It is difficult to overestimate the power and the passion that would go into the public response to successful attacks on American cities with weapons of mass destruction. It may be true, as some believe, that a moderated and measured response to such attacks is the best course for the United States, but it is almost impossible to imagine that this is the course Americans would actually follow.

One must also accept that others need to understand that Americans will respond to provocations like those of September 11 with massive and overwhelming force. Those who cannot stand us must learn at least to fear us.

Force remains an important element of international relations; America's enemies need to understand that the United States possesses more force than other powers and is, under the right circumstances, more than willing to use it. Frequently in the past other powers have misjudged the United States; we seem so feckless and indolent in peace that in both world wars and the Cold War our enemies seem to have discounted our will and ability to fight and persevere. Osama Bin Laden seems to have made this mistake; thanks to the Bush administration's response, others are less likely to repeat it.

This does not mean we must have a hard right-wing foreign policy or that only Republicans can govern the country. Presidents Truman and Kennedy rose successfully to the challenges of the Cold War. Some of America's most farsighted and sophisticated interventions in international politics were brought about because Jacksonians trusted leaders with complex, nuanced responses to urgent policy challenges. But this kind of public support can come only to leaders that the public trusts enough; it took a Nixon to get to China. Along these lines, the Bush administration's strategic decision to respond to September 11 as an act of war rather than as a crime was the only politically viable choice. If over a long period of time no new serious attacks appear, public concern could diminish, making other approaches viable, but that is not a realistic option until we have considerably more confidence in our homeland defense than would be justified today.

Although many of the benefits of victory were lost by grave mistakes that the administration made in the run-up to the war in Iraq, and again in the planning and execution of the postwar strategy, removing the regime of Saddam Hussein was a significant accomplishment.

By early 2004 the Bush policy in the Middle East was showing concrete results. The capture of Saddam Hussein has marked at least a temporary turning point in post-conflict Iraq; within weeks of his capture important Sunni leaders were calling for Sunni participation in the peace and reconstruction process and asking the remaining insurgents to lay down their arms. Muammar Qaddafi's surprise decision to dismantle his WMD program and accept spot inspections may have represented the culmination of a long process of political change in Libya. That process would never have started without Ronald Reagan's air strikes against Libya in 1986, and it is unlikely to have climaxed so soon and so completely without the demonstration of American power and resolve in Iraq. The European nations led by Germany who engaged Iran in the process that led to the Iranian agreement to accept weapons inspectors would never have taken this issue so seriously if they had not feared that the alternative to European demands was an American invasion. For years they had ignored American worries and requests on this subject; suddenly, in the spring of 2003 they began to act. Here, at least, Bush's policy of confrontation with "Old Europe" succeeded where earlier, more conciliatory administrations had failed. Syria, surrounded now by pro-American regimes in Israel, Turkey and Iraq, clearly understood that it could not count on its ties with France to protect it from American wrath. With the American military presence swiftly diminishing, the Saudi regime was both willing and able to confront its domestic extremists more vigorously than ever before. Deprived of much of their external support, and pressed continually by Israeli armed forces, Palestinian groups like Hamas did not, as was widely predicted, step up their bloody terrorist campaign against Israeli civilians. On the contrary, suicide bombings were becoming less frequent, and the openly terrorist factions among Palestinians were on the political defensive at home for the first time since the collapse of the Oslo process.

The Middle East is a volatile region and these promising developments might never come to fruition. But it remains clear that the invasion of Iraq created at least some of the strategic opportunities the Bush administration hoped for. Time will show whether the administration is up to the task of exploiting them.

Another big question that the Bush administration answered correctly has to do with the emerging relationship between Europe and the United States. While matters were not always handled well, the administration is right to believe that American foreign policy can no longer be Eurocentric. Despite the considerable political successes the Europeans have had in the construction of the European Union, and despite the great wealth and technological prowess these societies continue to show, Europe is unlikely to be the center of world politics in the twenty-first century. It is not simply that Europe is in demographic decline, that the remaining population is aging, that it has difficulties assimilating immigrants, and that its pension and medical obligations are ticking time bombs. The real factor driving the decline of Europe's prominence in world affairs will be the rapid development of the non-Western world, especially East and South Asia. Increasingly, the United States will be turning away from Europe toward new partners and, sometimes, new rivals in the developing world.

There will always be a special place in American foreign policy for our European allies, but they will have to learn to accept us for what we are. As long as we face the threat of grand terror, the United States cannot suppress its Jacksonian instincts, for example, in order to spare European sensibilities. Nor can we grant Europe a veto over American foreign policy, and if that is the price for Europe's help, we must learn from time to time to do without.

Ironically, turning away from Europe may be the best way to build a better relationship with it. Europeans have overestimated the political price the United States will pay for their help. Since the world remains a dangerous place, and Europe is unwilling (and perhaps unable) to arrange for its own defense without American involvement, it may be that in the future Europe will lower its price and place fewer demands on the United States than in the past.

It was brusquely done, and the timing was poor, but the administration was probably also right to dispel European illusions about the prospects that the United States would ratify the Kyoto Protocol, join the International Criminal Court as currently established, or more generally accept the European program of gradually subjecting America's freedom of action through institutions in which European states possessed one or more vetoes. While President Clinton was in the White House, the Senate rejected the Kyoto Protocol (by 95–0) and the Comprehensive Test Ban Treaty. There is no prospect that the Senate will ratify the treaty to establish the International Criminal Court in its present form.

Partly because it needed European cooperation in the Balkans, partly because ideologically many Clinton era officials agreed with European positions on issues like Kyoto and the ICC, and partly out of habits of consultation and deference that grew up during the cold war, the Clinton administration never quite made clear to Europeans just how unreasonable their hopes were. At the same time, most American diplomats and the broader "interlocutor class" of experts who specialize in transatlantic relations are generally more sympathetic to the European approach than they are to the red state, red meat approach of the American Jacksonians and the Revival Wilsonians who, since September 11, have figured so prominently in the politics of American foreign policy.

The Bush administration made the strategic decision that it no longer made sense to encourage Europe in illusions about the direction of American policy. Whether Europe liked that policy or disliked it was less important than that Europe understood it. Moreover, stroking Europe only seemed to increase Europe's already inflated sense of its importance in the world of American foreign policy. This transition was a necessary and normal one, and it ultimately does offer the prospect of a more realistic but still very close relationship among the Cold War allies. If the Clinton administration and the broader American foreign policy establishment had done a better job of communicating the changing American approach in earlier years, the transition might not have been so painful—but it is also true that the Bush administration could and should have done more to cushion the shock for what, after all, are some of our closest and most important allies in a dangerous world.

The bitterness of the controversy was regrettable, and hasty remarks by Bush officials exacerbated it, but it was probably on balance a good thing to remind Europeans in general and Germans in particular that transatlantic crises have a way of turning into European crises. With Germany, France, and Russia locked in an anti-American alliance, Poland understandably becomes nervous, and rightly so. When Russia and Germany get close, Poland has a way of getting smaller. A good German relationship with the United States remains the best basis for continuing progress toward European integration.

The shift away from institutions toward coalitions of the willing is another aspect of Bush administration policy that is likely to last. As they exist now, most (though by no means all) international institutions are deeply dysfunctional. The UN General Assembly, whose one-state–one-vote policy means that, officially in the UN system, India (population 1.07 billion) is more or less equal to Liechtenstein (population 33,000), has been completely irrelevant for decades.* The Security Council is increasingly crippled because, with three of the five veto-

---

* U.S. Census Bureau, International Database, Table 001, 2000, http://www.census.gov/ipc/www/idbprint.html.

wielding permanent members coming from Europe, it is too much of a retirement home for former world powers while major powers like India (with 17 percent of the world's population) and Japan (which accounts for 14.3 percent of world output)* are excluded. To be effective, institutions must reflect power realities; neither the Security Council nor the General Assembly now do.

The WTO has achieved what many political scientists might have thought impossible, and found an even more absurd and unworkable form of governance than the UN General Assembly. Carefully preserving the one-state–one-vote principle so that countries responsible for an infinitesimal proportion of world trade have equal weight with the trading superpowers whose policies actually matter, the WTO has added a political principle last enshrined in the eighteenth-century Polish Diet. Every member, however small and weak, can veto any agreement. The WTO is a perverse cross between the UN Security Council and the General Assembly. Let us hope that private industry never discovers that the votes and the vetoes of some WTO members just might be for sale.

But beyond the specific problems of specific institutions, there is a broader issue. International institutions, at least as we know them, are oriented toward achieving consensus through a process of deliberation, usually a very slow and thorough process of deliberation. The decisions they take are likely to be based on compromise, and whether they are security alliances like NATO or political organizations like the United Nations, there is a tendency to move at the speed of the slowest and most reluctant member.

Such institutions are very unlikely to provide the kind of rapid response that conditions in the twenty-first century will require. This is especially true of universal institutions like the UN or the WTO, institutions that

* From Table 1.1 (Size of the Economy) in 2003 *World Development Indicators* (Washington, D.C.: The World Book, 2003), 15.

aspire to include all states. The cultural and political divisions among human beings are too great for such institutions to be able to agree on more than a handful of issues, especially quickly. Inevitably, much of the work of the world will have to take place outside of—though not necessarily against—such institutions.

The Clinton administration went outside the UN system to fight the Yugoslav war over Kosovo; future American administrations may eschew some of the rhetoric that the Bush administration has used about international institutions, but no American president can ever accept a situation in which France pretends to an ability to veto American actions deemed necessary to the national security. Nor can future presidents entrust the defense of vital American interests to institutions that move at the pace of the slowest (and perhaps most anti-American) member.

Beyond these broad strategic decisions, there have been some other successes for the Bush administration, notably in Asia. After false starts with both China and the two Koreas, the Bush administration has managed some of our most difficult and important international relationships reasonably well. In particular, it deserves credit for working multilaterally—something many of its critics think it cannot do—to ensure as far as possible that there is a united front of concerned countries pressing North Korea to resolve the questions over its nuclear program. As I write these words, it is not possible to tell whether Bush's effort to deter North Korea from developing a serious nuclear capacity without war will succeed. But to date the administration has kept the pressure up and kept a fractious coalition together.

Equally impressive, though widely unheralded by a public opinion with its attention fixed on the Middle East and Europe, is the way the Bush administration has achieved something that most administrations find very difficult: it has improved American relations with China without alienating Japan, and vice versa. It has also, despite fears in some quarters that it would send Taiwan misleading signals about American support for independence, managed the delicate task of Taiwan–mainland China diplomacy pretty well. As the economic ties across the Taiwan Straits grow, each passing year yields more reasons to hope that this difficult problem can be resolved peacefully to the satisfaction of both Taiwan and mainland China. One should also note that, with respect to China, the Bush administration has remained within the broad bipartisan consensus. It has built on one of the Clinton administration's most important accomplishments—China's entry into the World Trade Organization—and continued to press toward the stabilization and normalization of relations between what increasingly must be seen as the world's two most powerful countries.

Beyond that, it seems as if the reputation of the Bush administration for toughness and assertive defense of American interests, combined with a willingness to cooperate with China on issues of mutual interest, has laid the basis for a realistic and stable relationship between the two countries.

The administration has done reasonably well at managing the tricky task of improving American ties with India without causing a crisis in or losing the confidence of Pakistan. The specter of a nuclear war between these two countries has receded; the United States has won at least some cooperation from Pakistan in the war on terror and helped pressure it to reduce its support for terrorists in Kashmir. This was a difficult juggling act and the administration deserves more credit for its diplomatic dexterity in this case than it usually gets.

There are then some big decisions and matters that the Bush administration has gotten right, and which many of its critics have gotten wrong. But that is not the whole story. It is not just that the administration has made mistakes—it has, and some have been very costly. The Bush administration's conduct of affairs has been too choppy and uncertain, its ability to formulate and express its strategic direction too crude and unconvincing, and it has not yet found a way to articulate a positive agenda for the United States and the world that can win sympathy beyond our frontiers—or even beyond the ranks of the administration's conservative domestic supporters.

Some of this is to be expected. Not only was September 11 a major strategic challenge that forced American foreign policy to confront a range of new and difficult issues, but the new and even raw quality of the strategic thinking found among partisans of the various schools of the American Revival makes for a turbulent and frothy cocktail.

Genuinely new and original directions in foreign policy often start badly. Theodore Roosevelt and his colleagues left an important legacy in American foreign policy, but a surprising number of their key ideas turned out to be dead wrong. Even Theodore Roosevelt came to feel that the annexation of the Philippines, a signature issue for the imperialist movement, had been a colossal mistake. Writing in 1907, Roosevelt told William H. Taft that "the Philippines form our heel of Achilles. They are all that makes the present situation with Japan dangerous. . . . Personally I should be glad to see the islands made independent."* Similarly, Woodrow Wilson's Fourteen Points and League of Nations were the first real eruption of modern progressive internationalism into American foreign policy; few would now resist the conclusion that in many respects both the Points and the League were amateurish and unworkable, and that Wil-

* Theodore Roosevelt, *The Letters of Theodore Roosevelt*, ed. Elting E. Morison et al. (Cambridge, Mass: Harvard University Press, 1951–54), 5:761, quoted in Warren Zimmermann, *First Great Triumph* (New York: Farrar, Straus & Giroux, 2002), 445.

son's unsteady leadership led to serious and expensive blunders.

Yet over the next century much good has come from the ideas of both Roosevelt and Wilson. So the froth and spray of the first waves of a new version of American grand strategy do not determine where the tide is headed, and the mistakes do not invalidate the general movement. There is, it must always be remembered, no perfect foreign policy that solves all problems and costs nothing. The quest for perfection in foreign policy is even more hopeless than in domestic politics. To make policy is to make mistakes, and it is only to be expected that those trying to chart a new course should make more missteps than those content to stay on the old, well-traveled roads.

NINE

Where Angels Fear to Tread

While the Bush administration has gotten some important things right, it does not take a Metternich to notice that all is not well in the world of American foreign policy. Making all due allowances for the difficulty of the challenges, few impartial and fair-minded observers can resist the conclusion that not all of the administration's actions have had the desired results.

To start with, there are the tactical misfires that happen to every administration—the simple blunders, miscues, and general accidents that are far more common in every government (and in every business and private life) than most of us wish. These are sometimes important and can change the course of history, but there isn't much to be done about them but to list them, try to learn from them, and move on. One cost, however, of the kind of high-wire, high-risk foreign policy strategy that the Bush administration has chosen is that these kinds of mistakes can be even more expensive than usual when the time is short, the issues are hot, and the stakes are high.

Among the mistakes of this kind in the last three years we can count several intelligence and assessment errors. The most notorious and the most costly, of course, was the failure to better assess the state of Iraqi WMD programs under Saddam Hussein. There were some important nose-counting and vote-counting problems as well. The failure of a resolution in the Turkish parliament on March 1, 2003, to support the United States with troops in Iraq by a three-vote margin was an avoidable disaster. It certainly ought to have been possible to persuade the necessary swing voters to support the measure, and Turkish support before, during, and after the war would have made a major difference as events unfolded. (The failure to secure the approval of the U.S.-appointed Iraq Governing Council for a Turkish presence in Iraq after the war was a worse and even less excusable blunder.) It also seemed clear during the winter of 2002–2003 that as the debate on the second Security Council resolution over Iraq proceeded, the administration had a weak grasp of the sentiments of Council members. By delaying the quest for a second resolution for much of January and February the administration probably lost an opportunity to force a vote on a second resolution with a deadline which would have compelled France and its partners to put up or shut up. Once that window passed, the quest for a second resolution was likely to be a mistake unless the administration was sure of getting at least a majority of all members. Even if one or two permanent members had vetoed such a resolution, the administration would have had a strong argument that it was French rather than American unilateralism that was responsible for the lack of consensus on the Security Council. However, to seek such a majority of nonpermanent members and then fail to get it was perhaps the worst of all possible alternatives. The administration ended up looking desperate, isolated, and incompetent and highlighted its relative isolation when the attack went forward.

The most costly mistake the administration made in its first three years was a simple political one. Whatever one thinks of the war in Iraq, the way the administration went about preparing the public for the war and its aftermath was a disaster and will likely be studied long into the future as a classic example of how not to manage war policy. Not only did the administration lean too heavily on the possibility of weapons of mass destruction (and links to Al-Qaeda) when making its case for the war, but it utterly failed to prepare public opinion for the possibility (certainty) of a difficult postwar period. It is no doubt very tempting to hard-pressed politicians to sell wars on the cheap—to minimize the consequences and dangers. It is also undoubtedly true that many senior administration officials had themselves embraced the rosiest of scenarios for postwar Iraq. None of that excuses the failure to take elementary precautions against possible setbacks.

As a result, the aftermath of Bush's successful war in Iraq turned into the gravest challenge of his presidency up to that point. The failure to find weapons of mass destruction impugned his honesty and credibility; the period of chaos, anarchy, resistance, and American casualties that followed the war generated the deepest public doubts yet about his leadership and capacity to defend the United States.

Both were entirely avoidable. The administration could have made a more substantive and varied case for the war, and guarded against the possibility of mistaken intelligence reports without losing the necessary public support. It could also have issued much clearer and more dramatic warnings about the possible dangers along the way, especially in postwar Iraq. Winston Churchill's method is the best: promise blood, toil, tears, and sweat. If things work out better, good for you. But if there is trouble later, at least people do not lose confidence in your ability to assess the dangers and threats into which you are leading them. (The failure to plan better for postwar Iraq is a different kind of problem to be examined later.)

At least on this front, the administration appeared to be learning. No premature proclamations of victory accompanied the capture of Saddam Hussein in November, 2003. From the president down, administration officials spoke of a hard road ahead, with sacrifices and suffering still to come. The White House allowed Prime Minister Blair to break the news of Muammar Qaddafi's renunciation of his quest for weapons of mass destruction—and the White House conspicuously refrained from triumphalism in the wake of the announcement. Almost three years into its term of office, the Bush administration appeared to be learning the value of *gravitas*; unfortunately, it was an open question whether the administration could recover its lost credibility at home and abroad.

Relations with key American allies and partners suffered serious damage under the Bush administration. Certainly the administration misread the political situation in Europe and failed to find a way to prevent policy disagreements over Iraq from metastasizing into a full-fledged crisis of the Western alliance. As the crisis developed, the administration allowed France to get between Washington and Moscow, giving its European opponents more geopolitical weight than they would otherwise have had.

The administration fairly consistently misread the position of France by underrating its will to confront the United States over Iraq and its ability to make real trouble on the issue.

The contempt that many Americans feel for France is so deep that it often blinds them to the extraordinary intelligence and flair that the French at their best can bring to international relations. By 2002, French president Jacques Chirac had been longing for a grander position on the world stage since he informed the world in 1995 that because of Bill Clinton's weakness "the position of leader of the free world is vacant" and he nobly volunteered to fill that vacancy.* The fall of the USSR liberated France from fear of the superpower that had kept it unhappily in the American alliance during the Cold War. Immediately after the Soviets fell, a new nightmare emerged: united Germany. France conspired in vain with the Soviet Union to keep Germany divided; when that failed, France was worried that Germany might become a colossus, which would end France's dreams of dominating the European Union.

By 2002 it must have looked more and more to Paris that German unification was a failure, and that the Berlin republic was weak, indecisive, and far less able than France to adjust to the economic realities of a post-Fordist world. French diplomacy was running rings around the country bumpkins in Berlin, and for the first time in sixty years France felt free to engage in global diplomacy without worrying about its security at home.

French calculations changed again when German Chancellor Gerhard Schroeder, grasping for issues in the midst of a tight reelection campaign, announced that Germany would not support United States military action against Iraq. The stars were lining up for Jacques Chirac in a way that no twentieth century French leader could remember. In the Iraq crisis, Chirac had an opportunity that Charles de Gaulle longed for, but never saw: the chance to oppose the United States on a major international issue with strong German support. France had its best chance in decades to advance its long-term goal of defining a European foreign policy in opposition to American goals, and on an issue that would win France friends among the contract-dispensing oligarchs of the Arab world. Furthermore, the French position simultaneously pleased France's growing Arab minority and the

---

* Madeleine Albright, *Madame Secretary: A Memoir* (New York: Miramax, 2003), 186.

shady, sometimes anti-Semitic forces behind the Le Pen movement that represents a permanent threat to French center-right politicians like Chirac. Moreover, a strong and courageous stand against the Yankee menace would take public attention off his government's plan to introduce painful pension reforms as part of a longer-term strategy of economic adjustment away from *Fordisme*.

The Bush administration (like much of the American establishment) seems to have believed far too long that, as usual, France would pout, prance, and pirouette on the world stage as long as possible, but that ultimately it would side with the United States in Iraq (possibly in exchange for control over some portion of Iraq's oil and an appropriate cut of the contracts to be let by the new government). Unfortunately, as Schroeder's line continued to harden in the fall and as Russia continued to support the French position (both of which developments might have been avoided with a more adroit approach by the United States), Chirac's intoxication with his diplomatic opportunity reached a point at which the would-be leader of the free world was ready to play the role of Lucy in the old *Peanuts* comic strip. Speaking of the second Security Council resolution, Chirac said, "Whatever the circumstances, France will vote no." Whenever Charlie Brown tried to kick the football, any football, *La France* would pull it away.

One hopes that Chirac enjoyed this moment, because France's decision to block the second resolution may have been one of its worst mistakes since World War II. For most American opinion, including many who have serious reservations about the Bush policy, this was a decisive moment. Over time, it is likely that the United States will gradually and quietly take whatever opportunities arise—and they will come—to undermine France's tenuous place in the ranks of the great powers and to reduce its influence in Europe and beyond. As far as possible, the United States will make its most important decisions in rooms where the French have no seat. Revenge, it is said, is a dish best served cold, and the United States has a long memory.

This is a tragedy that should never have happened. Despite their differences, France and the United States are both better off when they can work together. For now, the damage appears so deep that little can be done to repair it. Those like me who believe that good Franco-American relations help promote the democratic values both countries share, must now wait for better times. Let us hope that they come.

Worse still was the damage to America's standing in Germany. Germany has disagreed with American policy before; for example, it was a strong critic of the Vietnam War. The disagreement over Iraq could and should have been managed in a way that would have minimized rather than maximized the collateral damage to the American-German relationship. It was not, and the Bush administration did more in three years to drive Germany into an anti-American bloc with France than Charles de Gaulle accomplished through a long and brilliant career.

Fortunately, the American position in Europe is a strong one. The Franco-German effort to commit Europe to oppose American policy in Iraq seems to have damaged French and German relations with the rest of the European Union more than it hurt the United States. The arrogance and unilateralism that both Paris and Berlin displayed during that crisis was a revelation to many of their neighbors, and their behavior over their joint failure to adhere to the terms of the stability pact underlying the euro in the fall of 2003 demonstrated a contempt for international institutions and the rule of law as shocking as anything American neoconservatives could dream of.

But if French and German arrogance and the natural divisions of jealousies of European politics meant that "Old Europe" could not create a durable new anti-American force in world politics, that did not make the Bush administration's European policy a success. "Divide

and rule" is a maxim that worked for the Bush administration in Europe, but the goal of American foreign policy
for about sixty years was to unite Europe and cooperate
with it. The Bush policy of dividing Europe into pro- and
anti-American blocs was a retreat from the longtime
American objective of shaping Europe into a force that
could help the United States advance democratic values
and the rule of law around the world. We are farther from
the goal of a united, vigorous, and cooperative Europe
than we were three years ago; future administrations will
need to work to repair the damage the unnecessarily
brusque and careless diplomacy of some members of the
Bush administration caused.

What the Bush team failed to realize is that Europe's
decline is a problem for American foreign policy, not an
opportunity. Europe's long demographic and (in relative
terms) economic decline, combined with its seeming
inability to maintain adequate defense forces means that
the United States can count on less help from countries
who share a great many of our core values. That increases
the costs and risks of America's world role.

At the same time, the bitter European resentment at
its declining world stature creates a political headache for
the United States. If, as we certainly were in the first two
years of the Bush administration, the United States is too
harsh and dismissive of Europe, America becomes an
easy scapegoat for Europe's festering discontent with its
place in the world. Europeans blame their diminished
clout on Washington's unilateralism rather than on bad
economic and political decisions that were made in
Europe, not America. This makes them less likely to
make better decisions that will reverse or at least slow
their future decline and reduces the chances that Europe
will rally to Washington's side with the considerable
resources and power that it still has. Economic reform
and foreign policy cooperation within the framework of
an intelligent though not uncritical engagement with
American foreign policy remains Europe's best choice.

American diplomacy should be making it easier for German and even French leaders to take this course; unfortunately, that is not the way things worked out in the first Bush administration. Future American presidents, even those who share the Bush team's basic assumptions about Europe's place in the world, will need to find a new and better way to engage with our key Cold War allies.

European policy does not, unfortunately, exhaust the catalog of the administration's costly diplomatic errors in managing relations with American allies. Europe was a noisy disaster for the Bush administration; Latin America was a quiet one. Perhaps the single greatest disappointment for Bush well-wishers was the administration's failure to follow through on the excellent beginning it made with Mexico. Bush said on September 5, 2001, that "the United States has no more important relationship than the one we have with Mexico."* Vicente Fox's Mexico, which once had high hopes of building a new kind of relationship with the United States, was grossly neglected after September 11.

Fox's top diplomatic priority—immigration accords with the United States that would have improved the lives of Mexicans seeking temporary work north of the border—was much harder to realize after September 11 sensitized American opinion to the importance of border security and as the recession focused attention on low-wage competition from immigrant labor. Bush moved in this direction in early 2004, but it was too little, too late. The United States should have done much more to support Fox in the early years of his presidency. We may have missed a rare opportunity to make a historic difference in an important relationship, and the dangers to the still fragile institutions of Mexico's democracy and civil society remain very real.

* The White House, *Weekly Compilation of Presidential Documents* (Washington, D.C.: Government Printing Office, September 10, 2001).

Throughout the Western Hemisphere the Bush record provides little to cheer about. Support for the abortive coup against Venezuelan president Hugo Chavez embarrassed the United States and gave its enemies reason to question the sincerity of its support of democracy in the hemisphere without succeeding in helping Venezuela climb out of the hole that Chavez and his opposition were digging for it. Pro-American governments in both Argentina and Brazil were replaced by governments that sought to distance themselves both from the Bush administration and from American economic and political goals generally. Negotiations for the Free Trade Area of the Americas (FTAA) foundered; by November 2003, the ministerial meeting on the FTAA in Miami was forced to dramatically scale back expectations for the kind of agreement that could be reached.

Overall, it was in its public diplomacy that the Bush administration suffered the most consistent record of setbacks and defeats. There is no need to assemble and belabor the extensive and well-reported polling and other evidence here; not since the height of the Vietnam War, if then, has the United States been so unpopular with so many important audiences in so many countries. Right or wrong on the substance, the Bush administration has completely failed to make its case to world opinion, and the effect of this ongoing and serious failure has been to provide aid and comfort to our enemies and to complicate virtually all of the tasks of American foreign policy. The consequences of this disastrous performance will linger into the future; some of the damage that America's image overseas suffered in the first three years of the Bush administration will not be quickly or easily repaired.

Bush's harshest critics had an easy explanation for the failed public diplomacy: Bush's foreign policy was deeply unpopular around the world because it was a terrible foreign policy, and Bush's public diplomacy was doomed to failure because while you can put a pretty pink ribbon on a dead cat, you can't make a market for it.

From my own experience of speaking about American foreign policy to dozens of audiences and over a wide range of media outlets in Europe, Asia, Latin America, and the Middle East in the last three years, I can say confidently that the situation is a good deal more complex than this. When given a real chance to hear and discuss the perspectives shaping American foreign policy, foreign audiences do often become more sympathetic. The criticism does not go away entirely, and some foreigners, just like some Americans, will never support anything the Bush administration does—but over and over again I have seen bitter alienation and antagonism change into more complex and nuanced feelings as international audiences become more aware of the range of considerations and goals that shape America's national strategy. Yet foreign students, businesspeople, media commentators, and even in some cases foreign policy experts tell me after many of these talks that this was their first opportunity to hear a serious and measured explanation of American foreign policy in the post–9/11 world.

While there are often very specific local issues that influence the way various audiences react to American foreign policy in different parts of the world, there do seem to be some common factors behind the inability of the United States to get a hearing for its side of the story around the world today. To begin with, during the 1990s both Republicans and Democrats in the Congress slashed spending on public diplomacy. If history was over, why maintain libraries, study centers, and speakers' programs around the world to explain American society and American foreign policy? The United States Information Agency, an agency that had specialized in public diplomacy, was folded into the State Department and this, many observers feel, has substantially reduced the effectiveness of our outreach. These programs were built up during the Cold War because American policy makers believed that our foreign policy objectives could not be reached without a broad public diplomacy that helped create a favorable or at least understanding climate of opinion about American foreign policy around the world. After September 11 when we once again needed this support, we did not have the people, the programs, or the resources to engage constructively with public opinion in much of the world.

The absence of an infrastructure to build understanding of American foreign policy was particularly damaging given both the dramatic changes in American foreign policy both before and after September 11—and also given the strategic decision apparently made by at least part of the Bush administration that it was more important to frighten and overawe potential adversaries than to reassure friends or win over doubters. Very harsh and dramatic statements by high-ranking officials aimed at deterring hostile governments from collaborating with our enemies often had the effect of confusing, alienating, and alarming friends and potential friends. At the same time, Europeans and others were largely unprepared for the Jacksonian element in our national character and did not know what to make of its sudden reappearance in our foreign policy.

But the most important failures in American public diplomacy took place at the level of elite communication rather than mass communication. During the Cold War, and even subsequently, the political elites of American allies performed a critical task that Americans cannot do: they argued the case for the American alliance and for cooperating with the United States in their own countries. Their political skills, their understanding of their own cultures, their institutional power, and the respect in which they were held by their fellow citizens enabled leaders like Konrad Adenauer to bring Germany into the Western alliance. Out of conviction that American leadership was a positive good for their own countries, politicians, journalists, novelists, essayists, university professors, labor leaders, and many others spontaneously came to the defense of the United States and the American alliance. Even when from time to time such leaders disagreed with specific aspects of American policy, they were a force for mutual understanding, for limiting the fallout of policy disagreements and, in the last analysis, for doing the hard and necessary work to keep the alliances strong.

What, more than anything else, has crippled the public diplomacy efforts of the Bush administration is that in many countries we have at least temporarily suffered a "secession of elites"—a loss of support from this key class of opinion leaders. This is not true everywhere in the world; in eastern and southern Europe, for example, while public opinion often did not support American policy in Iraq on the merits, local leaders were able to win public tolerance of policies in support of the United States. Almost single handed and at great political cost, Prime Minister Blair fulfilled the responsibilities of this role in Great Britain. But in much of Latin America, East Asia, the Middle East, and certainly in "old Europe," the United States can no longer count on the high levels of support from elites that it once had. Without a strong local base of trusted figures who advance pro-American ideas on their own, the United States will find it very hard to gain the kind of support an active foreign policy—any active foreign policy, not just the current one—requires.

It is far too simplistic to blame this secession on the Iraq crisis. In Korea the secession is generational; a younger generation of Koreans resents past American support for military governments and is less concerned about North Korean aggression than the continuing presence of American troops on the peninsula. (South Korea, of course, has supported American policy in Iraq and sent troops to that country.) In Latin America, a very disturbing decline in elite support for the United States reflects disillusionment with the consequences of American trade and economic policy in the 1990s. Always and everywhere, elite support for the United States has been badly eroded where elites fear that the global, market-driven capitalism the United States now promotes will weaken their positions.

But if the foreign policy of the Bush administration cannot be entirely blamed for the ongoing secession of elites from the American project, the administration must certainly accept some responsibility for failing to prepare for it and, where possible, to reverse the trend or at least palliate its effects. These failures had very significant practical consequences for the Bush administration and help explain some of the failures it encountered at the United Nations and elsewhere as it tried to reenergize the old American alliances for the war on terror.

The secession of elites is a problem that future administrations will need to address with more care. It is a dangerous trend, and ways need to be found to reverse it.

Trying to get at the root causes of some of the Bush administration's foreign policy problems is more than an interesting intellectual exercise. It took office as an ambitious, talented, and deeply serious administration whose leadership included some of the brightest and most accomplished figures in the country. Forces and ideas that will be shaping our foreign policy for the next generation tried their wings in this administration.

Some of its most expensive foreign policy failures seem to be directly related to the difficulties of holding its vibrant but combustible coalition together. The extraordinary and even mind-boggling failure to plan more adequately for postwar Iraq appears to have resulted in part from the suspicion and hostility among different factions in the administration. The neoconservatives did not want compromising realist bureaucrats in the State Department organizing the postwar government, but the neoconservatives in the civilian leadership of a Pentagon allergic to nation-building lacked the bench depth and resources to make serious plans. The poor presentation of the case for the war also seems to have reflected an unhappy lowest-common-denominator compromise among the different ideological strains of the governing coalition.

Not even the most committed defenders of the Bush administration try very hard to justify the series of policy missteps and missed opportunities that marked the early months of the coalition presence in Iraq. The failure to plan better for the restoration of order and the repair of infrastructure gave opportunities to Saddam's loyalists— who initially were stunned by the speed and complete-ness of the regime's collapse—to build a resistance to the occupation. These failures cost the United States consid-erable good will among ordinary Iraqis and through-out the wider Arab world. They are the less excusable because the experiences in Afghanistan had already given policy makers opportunities to appreciate some of the difficulties involved in the occupation and pacification of a large state. The Bush administration ended up carrying out the best possible policy in Iraq—removing Saddam from power followed by support for a new and more democratic Iraqi government—in almost the worst possi-ble way.

It is particularly painful to note that the individuals most responsible for these planning failures are found on the neoconservative wing of the Bush administration. This is the group who put the most importance on the struggle in Iraq as the beginning of a democratic transfor-mation of the entire Middle East. They were also strong and sincere supporters of the view that intervention in Iraq was justified on humanitarian grounds: the suffer-ings of the Iraqi people under the Saddam regime were truly intolerable. That people holding these views should then fail so abysmally to understand the challenges before them, and to take proper steps to meet them, is extraordinary.

Most of the criticisms that non-neoconservatives make of these Revival Wilsonians are ideological in nature: their critics think they should care more about the United Nations or European allies or global warming than they do. But the failures of the occupation in Iraq are a different kind of failure: this is a case in which the neoconservatives identified a major strategic goal and then botched the job of reaching it.

Fortunately for the United States, Iraq, and the entire world, these failures seem to have been damaging but not decisive. Policy chaos created unnecessary difficulties and damaged American credibility. It has not yet doomed the intervention to failure. One can only hope that those responsible for this mess will reflect deeply on their failures and that, if the United States should ever again find itself undertaking responsibilities comparable to those we now face in Iraq, the officials directly responsible for shaping the effort will rise better to the occasion.

The administration was only partly successful in managing one of the classic problems of American foreign policy. Long, complex wars cannot be fought without strong Jacksonian support, but Jacksonian ideas about strategy and tactics do not always fit the constraints imposed by the international situation. Lyndon Johnson could not invade North Vietnam or blockade its harbors to prevent the resupply of enemy forces in the South. Harry Truman could neither "unleash Chiang Kai-shek" nor otherwise turn the Korean conflict into a full-scale war with China. America cannot allow Iran and North Korea to get nuclear weapons, but using military force against these countries poses some very difficult issues. Bush could not tolerate Al-Qaeda activity, but there are limits to how aggressively he could pursue it in various countries of the Arab world. Terrorism cannot be tolerated, but the United States needs an Israeli-Palestinian peace process at some point.

Additionally, Jacksonians do not like nation-building and they do not like spending money or losing soldiers in foreign countries. Once Saddam was overthrown in Iraq, and especially when the much ballyhooed weapons of mass destruction remained vexingly elusive, Jacksonians began to lose enthusiasm for having American troops shot while guarding checkpoints and intersections. The idea of spending tens of billions of U.S. taxpayer dollars—at a time of economic hardship and spiraling deficits at home—on the reconstruction of the country with the world's second largest oil reserves does not fill Jacksonians with joyful enthusiasm. News that the Bush administration wanted funding to establish postal codes in Iraq roused Jacksonian opposition to meaningless foreign giveaways. Surely the country with the world's second largest oil reserves can pay for its own post office, they reasoned.

Jacksonians can be convinced that the United States must prevail at all costs in Iraq, and they can be persuaded, with difficulty, that money must accompany U.S. troops, but this is not the sort of war they had in mind. The realization that the neoconservatives see the work of reconstruction and occupation as, potentially, a model for the entire Middle East makes Jacksonians edgy and uncomfortable.

It is a perennial problem in American foreign policy that Wilsonians often write checks that Jacksonians do not want to cash. This is one of the many ways in which the neoconservative Wilsonians resemble the old, pro-UN and pro-humanitarian intervention variety.

Adding to the difficulties of the administration was the degree to which both the Revival Wilsonian and populist nationalist or Jacksonian elements within it do not have a long history of government responsibility. Neoconservatives have held high office in past administrations, but the combination of the political instincts of the president and the political climate after September 11 gave them an unprecedented chance to take their ideas out of the think tanks and briefing books and test them in the field. It is a famous maxim in military science that no battle plan survives contact with the enemy; neoconservatives discovered in Iraq what partisans of other foreign policy doctrines had learned in previous administrations about the vulnerability of foreign policy doctrines and abstract ideas to events in the field. It seems likely that many neoconservatives will emerge from the policy wars over Iraq with a new and healthy respect for the complexity and contingency of events.

Among both Democrats and Republicans today, the conventional wisdom holds that the foreign policy of the George W. Bush administration has little in common with the policies pursued under President Clinton. Yet this wisdom overlooks some basic facts. For one thing, both the former president and the current Senator Clinton have been among the most sympathetic Democratic observers of the Bush administration policy, offering the current president important support on the question of the dangers posed by the Saddam Hussein regime in Iraq.

In many ways, the two administrations are joined at the hip, and both the greatest achievements and greatest problems of the Bush administration reflect the failures and successes of the Clinton presidency. The strong support from central Europe for the war in Iraq, support which effectively blocked the Franco-German effort to rally Europe against the United States, reflects the close relationships that grew up between the United States and countries like Poland during the Clinton administration's far-sighted effort to expand NATO eastward. Without the success of the Clinton administration in bringing China into the WTO and giving China permanent access to the American market, it is unlikely that the Bush administration would have been as successful in solidifying the Sino-American relationship after September 11. The realistic and practical relationship between the United States and Russia under Bush is also a continuation of the pattern established during the Clinton presidency.

Bush's most acute problems came from areas and issues where Clinton's foreign policy was less successful. The Clinton administration's agreement with North Korea was not, alas, sufficiently verifiable to stop the regime's progress toward nuclear weapons. The political fallout from the Asian financial crisis in 1997–98 left the United States with severely damaged relationships with Indonesia, South Korea, and Malaysia. The ease with which Al-Qaeda sympathizers were able to operate in Indonesia, in particular, was partly a result of the economic collapse, partly a result of the political collapse of the Suharto regime, and partly reflected public bitterness and disillusion with the American response to the financial crisis. The economic crisis also helped crystallize anti-American nationalist sentiment among many younger South Koreans. And while, fortunately, the problems in Latin America, including Venezuela and Colombia, did not blow up in the first years of the Bush presidency, the failures of Clinton policy in Latin America set the stage for important challenges in the future there.

Above all, the issues facing the Bush administration in the Middle East were as serious as they were because of Clinton's failures to deal effectively with Al-Qaeda and Saddam Hussein, and because the collapse of the Oslo peace process left both Palestinians and Israelis embittered and distrustful.

Beyond this, it was the assumptions shared by the two administrations that contributed to many of the Bush administration's greatest problems. In the Introduction, I wrote about the American conviction in the nineties that we had become an irresistible nation and that history had ended with the collapse of the Soviet Union. Both the Clinton and the Bush administrations shared this perspective, and it was slow to disappear even after the shock of September 11. Although members of the Bush administration had criticized what they saw as the carelessness and disregard for national strength of the Clinton years, it is difficult to avoid the conclusion that this behavior continued after Bush's inauguration. Before September 11, the Bush administration paid little attention to the views of other countries—partly out of a reckless conviction that we would never need their help. After September 11, the administration was still prone to overplay its hand and to assume that other countries had no choice but to follow America's lead.

For all its talk about American power, the Bush administration sometimes seemed to have little idea how to get things done with it. Worse, it seemed to have little idea just how limited its persuasive power actually had become. Repeatedly the Bush administration allowed itself to get out on a limb asking for help—votes in the Security Council, troops or financial help in Iraq—and then suffer humiliating public rejection as country after country defied American pressure and discovered that there was little the United States could do to respond. The appearance and reputation of power is an important part of its substance; exposing the United States to repeated public rebuffs has actually undermined America's reputation and therefore its power on Bush's watch.

At times the Bush administration looked like the Wizard of Oz bellowing, "Pay no attention to that man behind the curtain!" The bellows heave, the thunder roars, the smoke boils, and the lights flash—but the power to inspire awe and obedience has departed. The Bush administration was too often like a man who has just traded up from a compact to an SUV and figures that because he now has a larger, more powerful vehicle, he can venture much more boldly and aggressively out on the lake ice. Not only was our vehicle heavier, the change of seasons (from Fordism to millennial capitalism, to stretch the metaphor) was unleashing forces that weakened the ice, the political support for the United States, on which the administration needed to drive.

At other times it is not that the new American stance in the world exacerbates problems, but we have not yet managed to develop new, positive American Revival–based approaches to the problems inherent in the American project. In one sense this means we need more American Revival thinking, not less, to overcome problems that critics have seen, but at the same time we need more realistic American Revival thinking that does not assume that all our problems will melt into air if we just assert ourselves forcefully enough.

To see why, one can look at the consequences for American foreign policy of the rise of the neoconservatives—an important and in many ways a benign development in American foreign policy that has, however, in some ways made the task of American foreign policy harder, not easier. The Middle East is an obvious example, where the avowed intention of the neoconservatives to push toward democratization is deeply unsettling to some of our older allies, like the far from democratic governments of Egypt and Saudi Arabia. Neoconservative foreign policy puts the United States on a high-risk, high-stakes course in the Middle East, but because neoconservatives openly scorn old Wilsonian institutions like the United Nations and the powers of "old Europe" the United States can find itself alone and isolated when the high-profile, high-risk neoconservative policy goes awry, as in postwar Iraq.

More strength and more stress: the American Revival is bringing us both. At home the American Revival stands for, among other things, an intensification and acceleration of America's ongoing capitalist development. By removing barriers and regulations and promoting business-friendly policy and the continued development of capital markets, American Revival policy makers offer the inner logic of capitalism more opportunity than ever to transform American life. If the history of the last three hundred years can teach us anything, it is that this opening will not only usher in a new era of American innovation, prosperity, and power, it will also usher in waves of social unrest and difficulty for other countries around the world. The American Revival is going to increase the revolutionary tension associated with capitalism; this will lead to more problems for American foreign policy, even as it increases the resources of the United States and its relative power to deal with them.

The United States is not going to slow down its capitalist development to avoid offending the sensitivities of foreign countries and it probably could not even if it tried. What this means for American foreign policy is that even as the resources and relative strength of the United States continue to grow, the country is going to have to work harder to overcome resistance and resentment springing from ways in which American business practices, corporations, and strategies affect the domestic development of other countries, forcing them to choose between unpopular social and economic changes or falling further behind the American colossus. The consequences of this will be part of what the United States has to deal with—volatility, economic upheavals and political unrest, anti-American and antiglobalization activity in both first and third world countries—and will contribute to what is likely to be a serious legitimacy crisis for the American system.

We should never forget that the United States is provoking a revolution in its own system. The strongest power in the world is getting stronger, or at least thinks it is. That inevitably sets off a current of cascading disturbances in international society as other countries adjust to the new posture of the United States and decide what to do in response. Change always poses problems for hegemonic powers, even when the change is caused by the increasing strength of the hegemon. The American Revival movement in our foreign policy grows out of a sense that the world and the United States are in a period of rapid, deep change: we need to reflect much more deeply than we have yet done on how our foreign policy should respond to the mighty forces that are being unleashed in our system.

As the shift to millennial capitalism and the acceleration of technological progress move forward, the increasing power of the United States combines with the increased level of threat to exacerbate the basic contradiction in the global system. Is this a world order in which all states have an equal stake, or is it an American empire that the United States imposes on others? In reality, the American project is and will remain an uneasy combination of the two. It is an order that rests on power, and managing the balance between these two aspects of the world system is one of the most delicate and critical tasks American policy makers must address.

After September 11 the Bush administration lost control of this balance. The administration was unable to counter hostile propaganda, fueled by real questions and concerns, that its new doctrines of preemptive warfare and unilateral action represented a decisive shift in American policy toward the creation of an empire that would, naturally and obviously, threaten the independence and interests of other countries in all parts of the world. A perfectly justifiable military action against the rogue regime in Iraq was effectively and widely portrayed as an assault by the United States against the foundations of international order.

The administration also lost control in managing America's role in the conflict between Israel and the Palestinians. The United States must stand behind Israel and support its right to exist, but it must also be seen to support the legitimate aims of the Palestinians. Bush went further than any previous U.S. president in supporting the Palestinian right to statehood, but without a stronger U.S. response to shortsighted Israeli policies, these concessions had little effect on Palestinian or Arab opinion. Managing these relationships is one of the toughest tests American presidents face; unfortunately the costs of failure are high. Future administrations will have to make up the ground lost under Bush.

I would not want to end this criticism of the administration without noting that it is much easier to sit back at leisure to critique American foreign policy than it is to run it, especially when the American project faces unprecedented economic, political, and military challenges that nobody fully grasps or understands. The summer of 1864 found Abraham Lincoln criticized for having no strategy for winning the Civil War and fighting an uphill campaign for reelection against a popular general, George B. McClellan, on the Democratic ticket. Neither Winston Churchill nor Franklin Roosevelt covered themselves with glory during the first phase of their wartime leadership.

One must also recognize that Bush's domestic opponents have not covered themselves in foreign-policy glory. Even in the darkest hours of the Bush presidency— when Saddam was still free and casualties among coalition forces in Iraq were approaching one hundred a month—polls continued to show that the American people trusted the Bush administration more than the Democrats on national security. This was both a testimony to Bush's ability to craft a foreign policy that resonated with the political and moral instincts of the American people and evidence that the opposition had not yet managed to present a cogent and convincing alternative strategy. If there is one lesson we should all take from September 11 and the war on terror, it is that foreign policy is hard. It is hard to plan and execute it well, and it is almost as hard to oppose a foreign policy effectively, intelligently, and sensibly.

No matter who is in the White House, the coming

years are likely to see a difficult international environment. Americans expect and deserve a candid discussion of their wartime leadership. The Bush administration recognized and vigorously responded to the greatest security challenge the United States faced since the height of the Cold War. It successfully launched a counterattack against Al-Qaeda centers in Afghanistan; by removing Saddam Hussein it lanced a boil that was infecting the entire region and created an opportunity for a new and more stable future in the region. Yet these brave and bold policies were carried out in ways that deprived victory of much of its value. The administration was unable to convince much of world public opinion to share its assessment of the danger of Saddam Hussein, and much of that support evaporated when the intelligence on Saddam's WMD program was found to be faulty. The administration utterly failed to develop and implement a coherent plan for postwar Iraq, with consequences that cannot fully be comprehended even today. The price for its victories was what may turn out to be long-term and lasting damage to some of America's key Cold War alliances. And even as the Bush administration continued to protect the most important asset for any administration leading this country in war, the confidence of a majority of the American people, its conduct of foreign policy was polarizing the body politic to a dangerous degree.

One can only hope that in its remaining time in office, long or short, the Bush administration will keep its strategic vision, acquire more tactical skill, and build a broader national and international consensus for its policies. Without some improvement in execution and consensus building, history's judgment will likely be harsh.

PART FOUR

The Future of American Foreign Policy

TEN

Fighting Terror

Americans faced two challenges in the late 1940s. On the one hand, we had to stop the spread of communism across Europe and Asia while containing the military power of the Soviet Union. On the other, we had to replace the British world system with a new set of political and economic institutions and practices. If containment had failed and communism had spread across the world, the new economic system and our alliance network would have been a useless failure. If our economic and political system had failed, communism and Soviet power would have spread across a bitter, impoverished world.

We are once again fighting a war on two fronts. On the one hand, we must deal with the challenge of fanatical terrorists prepared to wage total war against us with weapons of mass destruction. At the same time, we must repair the damage to the American system and find a way to manage the American project under new and in some ways less favorable economic and political conditions. If we fail to deal with the terrorists, the global economy and political order may well collapse in apocalyptic ruin. If we fail to build an economic and social system that satisfies enough of the needs of enough of the world's people, then the terrorists will continue to recruit new allies as our old friends fall away or turn into enemies or cold, impassive neutrals.

Either way, we lose, and billions will suffer and many will die in the ensuing chaos, poverty, misery, and destruction.

Some observers think that the two conflicts are less interdependent than this. Noting that the suicide terrorists of September 11 came mostly from relatively privileged families in Saudi Arabia—by no means the poorest of the world's developing countries—these writers argue that easing world poverty is not a requirement for ending world terror.

This is partly true and partly false. The link between poverty and terrorism is not a simple one: the world's poorest people do not become the world's most dangerous terrorists. This is not something new: the most dangerous communist leaders were often, like Lenin, from relatively privileged and educated families. Stalin was a seminary student in his youth, not a starving peasant eking out a meager existence in the fields. Ho Chi Minh attended the prestigious National Academy in Hue and traveled to London and Paris. Fidel Castro, the son of a wealthy sugar plantation owner, was educated at a prestigious Jesuit academy and obtained his law degree. Che Guevara came from the Argentine middle class and had a medical degree.

What is true, however, is that societies in social, political, and economic crisis breed radical ideologies and create a public opinion that is receptive to totalitarian values and ideas. The upheavals, displacements, sufferings, anxieties, and disappointments of life in industrializing Europe and Russia not only helped shape communist and fascist theories, but such social problems made millions of Europeans receptive to totalitarian appeals.

Furthermore, the disorders and failures of a capitalist system in crisis weakened the forces of order. The business and cultural elites that could have helped stabilize

Weimar Germany were crippled by postwar inflation. The poverty and misery of post–World War II Italy and France greatly strengthened the position of the communist parties of those two countries while undermining the will and the ability of the anticommunists to defend themselves. The consolidation of democracy in post-communist Russia has clearly been hampered by the failure to create an orderly, prosperous economy.

A new factor today makes these problems more urgent: failed states. Governments that cannot police their territory—where government authority does not penetrate into the backcountry or where swollen urban slums create large and unpoliced zones under the authority of criminal gangs—pose serious security risks in a world where terrorists are looking for safe havens and bases.

What all this means is that unless the United States and its allies find ways to promote orderly and peaceful development in much of the world, the ideologies and organizations of terror will flourish and our security at home will be endangered.

The final chapter deals with these broader challenges, but the first and most urgent task facing the United States is to cope with grand terror. To cope successfully with the threat of grand terror, we must begin by accepting that this is a war: that despite the unconventional nature of the threat and of our opponent, the radical new form of fascism championed by men like Bin Laden and supported by organizations like Al-Qaeda is a fundamental challenge to our lives, our values, our freedoms, and to everything we have tried to create in the world. We did not seek this war and we do not want it; for years we did everything we could to convince ourselves that there was no war—no serious effort to destroy our society by violence and fear.

Time will tell, and relatively quickly, what kind of

threat the particular group of terrorists we now face is capable of posing. Yet even as we hope that the current challenge can be overcome in relatively short order, there is no prudent alternative to acting on the assumption that these groups can and will pose a significant threat for the foreseeable future. This is partly because we already have enough evidence of both their intentions and their capabilities to force us to tentatively assume that they are resilient and resourceful enough to continue to pose major threats. It is partly because even if we manage to defeat this particular group of terrorists in relatively short order we must still make the investments in political arrangements, security, and intelligence that can prevent new threats of this type from arising in the future. It is partly because the political realities of American life demand that our government take the fears and concerns of American citizens with due seriousness and respect. It is partly because so far we have erred far more often and more grievously by underestimating the terror threat than by overestimating it and, finally, it is partly because within very wide boundaries it is far more costly to err on the side of ignoring the terrorists than on the side of overpreparing for them.

Given all this, we need a way to articulate our grand strategy in the war on terror. We need a set of concepts that we can use to explain our policy to allied countries and to world public opinion; we also need a way to debate and discuss our grand strategy at home. In the Cold War, the concept of containing the Soviet Union and its communist ideology emerged at a relatively early date in the war and continued to describe American grand strategy through the fall of the Berlin Wall. The Cold War, like the war on terror, was something of a metaphorical war: once the Soviet Union acquired a large nuclear arsenal we did not have the option of settling the American-Soviet dispute by duking it out in the traditional manner of great powers.

The concept of containment helped bridge the gap between the deadly serious nature of the threat and the nontraditional foreign policy by which we met it. The goal was to destroy communism, but the method would not be a great power war. In George Kennan's analysis,* both communism and Soviet power depended on expansion for survival. If the United States could block the expansion of communism, the Soviet state would rot and decay from within, and ultimately crumble away. In the meantime, for forty years the concept of containment allowed American presidents and congresses to win public support for far-sighted, thoughtful policies that helped create a stable world order after the chaos of the first half of the twentieth century.

Not everybody in the United States accepted the idea of containment. Some preferred "rollback"—instead of holding the line and waiting relatively passively for communism to disappear on its own they wanted the United States to push it back wherever possible. Some thought that containment was too harsh and simplistic; they wanted the United States to live and let live—and, especially, not to intervene in developing countries to block the spread of communism. There were also debates among those who accepted the framework of containment on how to apply this grand strategy to particular circumstances. What kinds of nuclear arms limitation agreements, if any, were consistent with a containment policy? Did containment mean supporting South Vietnam against the North? Did it mean sending American troops to fight Marxist guerrillas in South America or Africa? Was trading with the Soviet Union consistent with a policy of containment, or did such trade strengthen the communists more than it helped us?

* "Sources of Soviet Conduct," *Foreign Affairs* 25, no. 4 (July 1947).

Containment was flexible enough as a strategy to serve us at times of great crisis—such as the Cuban Missile Crisis and the Berlin Crisis of the Kennedy years—but also in times of relative détente, as in the Nixon administration. When Soviet activism threatened to break the ring of containment, presidents were able to summon public support to hold the line. At other times, when the Soviet leadership seemed ready to live within the status quo that containment demanded, the United States was able to work with the Soviets to reduce the threat of superpower confrontation.

The containment policy that won the Cold War was actually a policy of triple containment. We sought first to contain the armed military power of the Soviet Union by building alliances against it, expanding our nuclear deterrent as needed and by maintaining a strong and credible presence in all the regions where it sought to expand. Second, we opposed the expansion of communist government throughout the world, even when the pro-communist forces were not those of the Soviet Union or its satellites. We supported Britain's successful guerrilla war in what is now Malaysia; we did what we could to block the spread of communism in Asia, Africa, and Latin America. We did not succeed in every case and in every country, but over the long forty years of Cold War our policy certainly reduced the ability of communism to conquer new territory. Finally, we opposed the expansion of communist and Soviet influence in the civil societies and political structures of friendly noncommunist states. The American labor movement worked with the American government as well as friendly foreign governments and labor leaders, for example, to stop the communist penetration of labor organizations in the United States and abroad. Anticommunist intellectuals and cultural figures consciously worked to provide an alternative to and combat the influence of the often large and intimidating presence of communist cultural and intellectual leaders in various parts of the world. We also made considerable investments in giving local anti-communist and noncommunist leaders the skills and support they needed to help keep their own societies free of this blight.

As we search for an equally useful and flexible strategic framework to organize and mobilize for the war on terror, I think we could do worse than update the old concept of containment for this new kind of war. Like the Cold War, our new war can't be settled in the old fashioned way. Al-Qaeda and the various organizations that loosely work with it are not a state; we will not defeat them by sending our armies against theirs. Like the Cold War, our new war will involve a whole series of military, intelligence, political, economic, and cultural activities. And also like the Cold War, our new war will probably include moments of relative quiet as well as times of great crisis, while requiring firm and patiently sustained long term resolve from the American people.

The concept of containment has another advantage: it is familiar to our Cold War allies and to the broader international community. One of the unfortunate side effects of the Bush administration's war policy has been to alarm and alienate some of our important past partners. One way to strengthen our alliances and update them for the new situation is to stress the continuities between our current policies and those of the past. Articulating our grand strategy in terms of containment stresses our firm and inflexible resolve to win this war, and it also stresses that we intend to use flexible, appropriate, and pragmatic strategies to fight it.

The new war is not a clone of the Cold War, and there will have to be differences in our strategic approach. A major difference is that deterrence does not operate in the same way in the war on terror as it did in the Cold War. Because their motivations can be based in religious fantasy rather than conventional power seeking, because terrorist leaders are hard to track and because their strength is not necessarily tied to that of a particular country, terrorists are not deterred by the American nuclear arsenal the way the Soviets were. On the brighter side, we are not deterred either; we are free to hunt them down and destroy their networks wherever we can. This could all change as the war evolves, but any new concept of containing the terror threat must include vigorous, unremitting, and direct attacks against terror organizations.

For all these reasons, we might do well to call our grand strategy in the war on terror "forward containment." It will include a version of the triple containment with which we defeated communism and the Soviet Union, but it will involve a much greater forward presence of the United States and a much greater willingness to engage militarily with enemy combatants on their own ground. We will seek through political and military measures to contain the danger that terrorists pose to the United States by weakening their organizations, cutting their ties to governments, and blocking their access to weapons of mass destruction. We will seek to contain the influence of the terrorist ideology. And we will contain the expansion and consolidation of state power by those embracing this ideology—we will resist any and all efforts to establish governments founded on these principles anywhere in the world—peacefully if we can, but if necessary through the use of force. Over time, we can reasonably hope that by depriving the terrorists of real victories, keeping their organizations weak, divided, and on the defensive, and building healthy societies in the Muslim world as elsewhere that can resist the blandishments of our enemies, we will deprive this movement of the oxygen it needs for survival. Bin Laden's style of hatred will be seen as one of history's dead ends and it will survive, if it survives at all, among isolated communities of alienated, powerless, and marginal misanthropes who may hate but do not dare or care to act on that hatred.

Most of the war on terror so far has involved the first kind of containment: moving to reduce the immediate danger that this movement poses to the U.S. homeland

and our citizens and interests abroad. Aggressively pursuing Al-Qaeda remnants in Afghanistan, continually upgrading our ability to interfere with their flow of funds, cutting them off from supporters, hunting down their remaining leaders, building more capable intelligence networks against the threat they present, restoring a healthy respect for America's ability and will to retaliate with overwhelming force against attacks: all this is already part of the war on terror and these efforts will continue and expand. The attacks of September 11 added new urgency to efforts to prevent proliferation and contain the dangers represented by the availability of "loose nukes" and materials for dirty bombs on the world's black markets. While pursuing Al-Qaeda and similar movements aggressively around the world, often in close cooperation with allies in Europe, Southeast Asia, and elsewhere around the world, we are upgrading and improving our homeland defenses and the security of key targets abroad such as embassies and military installations. We know that a defensive strategy can never be completely effective against terrorists who can choose their targets and their timing, but a combination of stronger defense with proactive methods to disrupt and harass their activities and reduce their access to the most dangerous types of weapons can significantly reduce their ability to cause harm.

The other vital aspect of this kind of containment is to cut the links between terrorist groups and governments. During the Cold War international society turned a blind eye to the practice of states maintaining links with terror groups. Countries like East Germany and Syria were openly and flagrantly sheltering terrorists and, in many cases, there were strong links between their security services and these groups. The Arab-Israeli conflict was another force tending to legitimize this practice in the eyes of some states; support for Palestinian groups, even those that used attacks on innocent civilians as their primary tactic, became a normal thing in parts of the world.

The collapse of the Soviet Union ended the practice of European states sponsoring or linking with terror groups, but in the Middle East the practice persists. This practice must stop. It is no longer tolerable in an age of mass terror. Countries that allow their territory to host terror camps or even representation offices, and who knowingly allow their financial systems to be used to transfer and hold assets for terror groups, are committing acts of war against civilization. Governments that offer bounties to the families of suicide bombers are committing an act of war. When American citizens are killed as a result of these actions, the U.S. government has the right and the duty to respond. (This does not mean that we should respond stupidly, counterproductively, or indiscriminately; we have the right to choose our own response and our own time, but these are acts we cannot ignore.)

It will probably also be necessary to end the disingenuous subterfuge of drawing artificial distinctions between the "civilian" and the "military" funding and arms of terror groups. Governments that supply funds to the "civilian" arms of murderous terror groups become accomplices to the acts of these groups; financial institutions that fail to exercise proper vigilance to make sure their facilities are not used to transfer money to murderers will probably face both civil and criminal penalties, as well as ruinous litigation from the families of those killed by the groups they have funded, as the mechanisms of the anti-terror campaign are more firmly and fully established.

As we go forward in this struggle it will probably be necessary to bring this principle again and again to center stage in international politics. Over time our goal should be to create a strong international consensus that sheltering and supporting terror is unacceptable. As that happens, sanctions and collective enforcement actions may be able to replace unilateral diplomacy backed by threats. Support from the United Nations helped force Libya to end state terrorism and compensate its victims. Governments that support terrorists in the future should know this could lead to military retaliation and to the jailing or execution of the officials responsible.

This problem will certainly entangle the United States in the contradictions of the international system. On the one hand, the principle that the United States will be seeking to establish and enforce—that states cannot support those trying to murder the citizens of other states— is a fundamental element of any serious system of international law. On the other hand, it is extremely unlikely that anything other than the exercise of American power, sometimes unilaterally, could ever make such a law effective. We cannot escape this paradox; the Parties of Heaven and Hell may combine against us, but we must nevertheless do our best both to uphold the concept of international law and defend the basic order that alone makes concepts like international law meaningful.

From the 1940s through the 1960s, the ideological power of communism was in some ways more dangerous than the military might of the Soviet Union. The ideas of communism rather than Soviet armies were on the march through western Europe, China, Latin America, and Southeast Asia in those years, and if the West had lost the Cold War it would have been because the ideas of capitalist democracies lost out in the ideological struggle to communism. The second dimension of our triple containment policy will probably involve containing the ideas of the terrorists.

Incidentally, this involves finding a better name for what we are opposing. "Islamicism" is an ugly term that also silently concedes that Bin Laden's ideology has a claim to be regarded as a legitimate form of Islam. We do not call the Catholic integralist ideology of those who supported Francisco Franco "Christianityism." We do not call the lunatic fringe of the Zionist movement "Jewism." I agree with Paul Berman's analysis in his book *Ter-*

ror and Liberalism that our enemies are fascists. "Arabian Fascism" is a totalitarian ideology inspired by a mythologized vision of the past. It does not attract Arabs only, but all those for whom the early Islamic wars of religion and conquest represent a golden age, and it aims by force to restore this past not only in the world of Islam, but ultimately throughout the world.

Arabian Fascism like the European Fascism of the twentieth century comes in two forms: secular and religious. Some of the European fascist movements, especially in Portugal, France, and Spain, were linked to parts of the Catholic church. Others, like the Nazis, were anti-Christian and either secular or neo-pagan. In the same way the totalitarian ideologies now tormenting the Muslim world include secular fascisms, like the Ba'ath Party of Iraq, and religious fascisms like that of Osama Bin Laden. Both movements believe in subordinating the rights and conscience of individuals and eliminating the independence of civil society in favor of a totalitarian politics to restore the exaggerated glories of a romanticized past. Both movements recognize no limits on the right of their leaders to command their followers to carry out lawless violence against innocent civilians. In European history, white was often the color of totalitarian movements claiming some kind of alignment with traditional religion—and people often spoke of a White Terror as opposed to the Red Terror of the Jacobins and Communists. Extending this language to the Middle East makes it possible to refer to the fascism of groups like Al-Qaeda as White Fascism; the term Black Fascism can be used for the secular fascism of leaders like Saddam Hussein. Both forms of fascism are deadly enemies of freedom and peace, and the United States and its allies should oppose them both, but the core of the present battle in the Middle East is the fight against the White Fascism of the Al-Qaeda fanatics, not the Black Fascism of the radical Ba'athists.

We must press the White Fascists ever harder toward

the fringes of public opinion in the Middle East and else-where, isolating and dividing them politically, even as we move to destroy their organizational capacity to harm us. This can be called "political containment." Accomplishing this effectively will require retooling and redirecting some of the ideological weapons the United States developed in the Cold War against communists. Just as we once learned to differentiate between left-wing Social Democrats and Communists, we will have to become much better at distinguishing White Fascism from conservative Islam. There are legitimate reasons pious and conservative Muslims might oppose American policies in the Middle East and elsewhere. It is perfectly understandable that not everybody in the Islamic world would welcome the intrusion of Western standards of dress, Western gender relations, and other forms of social change. One can understand that thoughtful people could take different views about the rights and wrongs of the dispute between the Palestinians and the Israelis. The United States can and should accept that those who oppose certain aspects of our presence and policies in the world may be our opponents, but not necessarily our enemies. Indeed, we can and should make common cause with legitimate Muslims against the common fascist enemy. If not even the royal family of the House of Saud meets the standards of the White Fascists, we are likely to find that hundreds of millions of other Muslims, extremely conservative and pious, also do not satisfy the fanatical demands of the Bin Ladenites. Democratic socialists were some of our most valuable allies in the campaign against communism; building bridges to the legitimately conservative as well as the more progressive currents within Islam will probably be part of the evolving American response to our new war. (We will similarly seek to separate legitimate and healthy nationalism in the Arab world from the toxic fumes of Black Fascism).

However slowly and with however many mistakes along the way, we are also likely to move toward a much

more effective intellectual, moral, and spiritual engagement with the Islamic world. Much of this will not come
from government, but from the independent, unguided,
and uncontrolled efforts of private citizens, religious
groups, foundations, universities, and other institutions.
Almost certainly Americans (along with Europeans and
many others) will move to promote intellectual and cultural openness in the Middle East by making more works
available in translation. Americans will work to build
closer academic ties and help more promising scholars in
the Middle East build international careers. The United
States has almost two centuries of experience in promoting education, especially education of women across the
Middle East; this tradition is likely to be revived and
enhanced. There is also likely to be much greater attention paid in the West to Islamic ideas and values, as well
as to the ideas and historical antecedents of Arabian Fascism. Americans are going to have to study the critiques
and the works of the new fascists as we once did the
works of Stalin, Lenin, and Marx. Unlike our increased
study of and appreciation for the spiritual and intellectual riches of authentic Islam, the study of the fascist
materials will not be for the fatuous purpose of appreciating the beauty and spiritual riches of these documents or
celebrating the diversity of those who want us dead; it
will and must be for the purpose of defeating fascism and
terror.

It appears likely that most Americans and most Muslims have an exaggerated sense of the philosophical and
political differences that divide us. In the Muslim world
the concept of the secular state took shape in the context
of the imposition by Kemal Atatürk and his less successful Arab imitators of the church and state model first
developed in Revolutionary France. In this Jacobin tradition, the state is hostile to the public expression of religious belief and seeks to limit the influence of religion in
the public square. Outward manifestations of religious
commitments—head scarves on schoolgirls in Turkey

and France, nuns and priests in clerical dress in revolutionary Mexico—are frowned on by aggressively secular states that have defined a fervent culture of popular religion as a potential source of rival and hostile power to the lay state. There is a rigorous attempt to confine the influence of religion to the private sphere and to introduce and follow civil codes that are rooted in, ultimately, Roman law rather than in either the religious feelings or the historic customs of the people.

Much of the populist reaction against secularism is from this point of view an understandable and even a commendable reaction against hostile attacks on religion by modernizing states on the model of Jacobin France. The American system, in which people are allowed and even encouraged to act on their religious beliefs in the public square, and where the state is more concerned to support the free expression of religion than to curb religious power and activity, is not part of the historical experience of the Muslim world. Slavishly imitating the American model is no answer to the real dilemmas Muslim peoples feel as they strive to reconcile their political institutions with their religious faith; but American ideas about a free religion in a free state are a potential point of contact between the societies, and there are more similarities between the religious policies of the early caliphs and the American people than are widely understood.

It is much too early to see how greater and more sympathetic study of the other in both parts of the world can find new points of contact, as well as clarifying the differences that do exist. The difference between contemporary American Christianity and the Christianity of the era of Muhammad developed because American Christians and their forebears came to agree with substantial elements of the Islamic critique of Byzantine Christianity as it existed in the time of the Prophet. If we look at the life of most American Christians today, we see a disdain for airy theological speculation and a commitment to practical works of charity and submission to God in a way that would have been pleasing to Muhammad and his early followers. Even Americans who belong to churches with religious hierarchies see their priests as teachers but not as a caste of human beings with special authority over their flocks—again, a criticism early Muslims made of the Christianity they knew firsthand. Christians have increasingly subjected their sacred texts and legendary lives of the saints to the critical scrutiny that the early Muslims gave to purported sayings of Muhammad. The Trinitarian piety of contemporary American Christians, though still something no Muslim could accept, is culturally much further from the pagan polytheism that, in the view of many Muslim scholars, tainted the monotheism of the Christians of earlier days. The concept of religious tolerance—and the duty of the state to protect people of many faiths—is a concept that Islam developed long before Christianity. It is related to another, even more profound Islamic contribution to the Abrahamic faiths: the idea that God is speaking through many religions, and that all the forms of God's prophetic revelation are entitled to respect.

Fears that the rise of more conservative and evangelical forms of Christianity in the United States will precipitate a war of civilizations seem somewhat overblown. The evangelical Protestant religious movement that has made such great progress in the United States in recent decades is much more flexible than many secularists and religious liberals are ready to acknowledge. The close relationship between conservative Jews and conservative Christians in American politics is one sign of this flexibility; so too is the close cooperation and fellowship that can be seen among conservative Catholics and Protestants in the right-to-life movement and elsewhere. This may look like the ecumenism of Hell to liberals, but it is both powerful and real. It was only in the last generation that conservative ecumenism made its appearance in American life; there is a real possibility that conservative

Muslims and Christians may also find new points of contact. In any case, the historic direction of American religion has been to retain its Christ-centered emphasis on rebirth and salvation while overcoming religious and ethnic bigotry; there is no reason to suppose that relations with Islam will not follow this pattern.

A richer and more authentic dialog of civilizations is likely to expand on this list of points of contact between the spiritual lives and concerns of Christians and Muslims in today's world. Getting to this point of understanding and respect will contribute to the isolation of the fanatical fascists in the Middle East—and reduce the political tensions between the mostly Christian West and the Muslim world by, in part, making the Christian world more sensitive to Muslim views and concerns.

The Cold War political struggle against communism, especially in its early period, challenged American society, and the rest of the West, to live up to its values more fully. Communist propaganda highlighted American racism, and the political fallout of this propaganda in the developing world was one of the factors that pushed American society in the Cold War era to fight against this ruinous legacy from an unhappy past. More broadly, capitalist society accepted the challenge of showing that it could do better than communism at improving the lives of working people and enhancing the lives of the poor.

We are likely to find that the struggle against White Fascism is going to bring similar moral challenges to which we must rise. Propaganda that the West has lost touch with its spiritual roots, that we have given our lives over to dissipation and an amoral search for pleasure, that our societies are depersonalized and uncaring, that we ruthlessly neglect the unfortunate in other, poorer countries, and that the exploitation of women continues under the mask of a philosophy of personal liberation: this kind of propaganda is as unfair and untrue as anything the communists used against us, but like a lot of communist propaganda it has some plausibility. As part of our grand strategy to isolate and contain Arabian Fascism we shall have to take steps to make these charges less plausible in the future. Inescapably, this will lead many Americans to renew their personal faith commitments and make the moral and social ideals of their religious roots more relevant in their daily conduct and in their assessments of politicians and of political ideas.

This second part of our containment strategy cannot succeed without addressing the Israeli-Palestinian conflict. There are few subjects of equal prominence in world politics about which so much has been written, and few subjects in which so much debate has yielded so little consensus or so little light.

Many observers believe that the best way to contain Arabian Fascism and relegate it to the lunatic fringe is to remove the just cause of much Arab ire: What they see as America's excessive and one-sided support for Israel. In this view, dealing with individual terror groups is attacking the superficial manifestations of our problem in the Middle East: the United States must deal with the "root causes" of the tension in the region, and once this is done, our other problems will become much more manageable. While American support for Israeli security may be acceptable, others add, the failure of the United States to pressure Israel on its policy of building settlements in the occupied territories and its security policies there is one of the chief causes of the anti-Americanism that finds its harshest and ultimate expression in terror attacks on American targets.

Ariel Sharon's policies exacerbated the conflict, and the Bush administration failed to pressure Israel. Nevertheless, European critics of America's perceived failure to deal with "root causes" in the Middle East should remember that European anti-Semitism and European imperialism are the root causes of most of the region's troubles. Europe persecuted its Jews for centuries, climaxing with the orgiastic horrors of the Nazi Holocaust.

Meanwhile, European empires divided up the Arab Middle East among themselves, inflicting grave wounds on Arab society. They designated Arab lands in Palestine for resettlement of Europe's desperate Jews, and now blandly lecture both sides on the need for patience and moderation—while complaining about America's efforts to clean up yet another mess that European imperialism left in its wake.

One must hope that future Israeli governments display more creativity and take more risks for peace than the Sharon administration has so far done; Americans must also take responsibility for the Bush administration's failure to engage more constructively. Nevertheless, when it comes to the Middle East, Americans sometimes think that Europeans have already done quite enough in this field and that the best thing Europe could do for the Jewish Question, as it used to be called, is to give it a rest.

The haste with which so many Europeans now rush to proclaim their moral superiority to Israel and compare every controversial act by Israeli security forces to the actions of Nazi storm troopers is, to American sensibilities, one of the less pleasing traits of some of our NATO allies. I do not believe this distressingly common tendency is, as some allege, simply the newest form of European anti-Semitism, but it is not innocent, attractive, or just.

But let us pass over these unhelpful recriminations and look at what we can and should do, alone and with our allies.

It is certainly true that a peace settlement between Israelis and Palestinians that is widely accepted as just and final in the Arab world would vastly improve the security and political situation in the Middle East and greatly simplify the task of dealing with Arabian Fascism.

It is, however, almost as certainly true that no such peace settlement will be reached anytime soon.

Although a minority in Israel is ideologically committed to the "Greater Israel" laid out in Deuteronomy, and powerful Israeli interests support annexation of significant parts of the West Bank, most Israelis want peace. Faced with a credible Palestinian offer on the basis of the pre-1967 cease-fire lines with minor adjustments, Israeli public opinion would almost certainly agree to the necessary territorial and political compromises.

The Palestinian equation is more complex. Many and possibly most Palestinians are ready to deal with Israel on this compromise, two-state basis, but moderates face resistance from many Palestinians who stand to gain very little from a compromise peace. A prosperous olive farmer has more to gain from peace than families crowded into the misery of the camps. Dispossessed refugees (including 2.5 million in Jordan, Lebanon and Syria) have little incentive to accept a peace settlement that neither gives them a right of return nor offers them compensation.* Radical opponents of peace can mobilize alienated, marginalized supporters and force moderates to pay a high price for supporting peace plans seen as insufficient. Without a functioning state and with no real democratic political process in place, it is difficult to measure public sentiment among Palestinians, or for the pro-peace elements of the leadership to impose an unpopular peace agreement.

Israeli hawks, some of whom have a vested interest in continued confrontation, can argue that the "Palestinian street" is not now and may not ever be ready for peace. And since in their current form, the territorial settlement offers little or nothing to most Palestinians, and since public opinion has become deeply embittered through years of conflict and occupation, these arguments simply cannot be dismissed.

---

* *Palestinian Territories*, The Economist Intelligence Unit (London: EIU Limited, 2003), 50.

As a result we face a dilemma. The Palestinian peace party cannot reliably deliver Palestinian society unless peace offers concrete benefits for the overwhelming majority of displaced Palestinians, and since there is no peace party in Israel if the return of millions of Palestinians is the price of a deal, peace remains tantalizingly out of reach.

In a situation where neither of the parties is willing to accept any of the feasible solutions, there is very little that an outside power can do to force an agreement. There are those who suggest that the United States should outline its preferred solution and then proceed to impose it by sending peacekeepers.

At some point some such solution might become feasible, but it is unlikely that such a move in the next few years would reduce anti-American feeling in the Middle East. Any settlement the Palestinians are likely to get, or the Americans (or even the Europeans) are likely to impose, is so far short of the minimum demands of a significant group of Palestinians that the peacekeeping forces will almost surely become the targets of new rounds of suicide bombers and other terrorists. The steps that the peacekeepers would need to take to protect themselves inevitably would be seen by many Palestinians and their supporters in the Arab world as further outrageous provocations by an America firmly in the pocket of the Zionist menace. Having American troops enforcing curfews, searching for weapons, operating military checkpoints on the West Bank, shooting people who attack them, and occasionally shooting innocent bystanders in the heat of battle and danger may not be the best way to improve America's public image in the Arab world.

Possibly we would achieve a settlement that terrorists on both sides would oppose, and then our troops would be bombed and shot at from both sides, as the British were in the 1940s. This hardly seems a formula for reducing tensions in the region, nor does it look like a policy that an American president could sell to the country.

This does not, I think, leave us quite helpless. It was very unfortunate that the Oslo peace process broke down in the waning days of the Clinton administration, and it has proven extremely difficult to get a replacement process under way in the poisonous atmosphere that the failure of Oslo left behind it. In time patient diplomacy can make some headway here, and with luck and skill we can hope to repair the worst of the damage.

Beyond that, it is probably time for the United States to concern itself much more directly with the state of the Palestinians. So far, the peace process has primarily concerned itself with the future of territory. The future of the people affected by the dispute, and especially the future of displaced Palestinians, has not been addressed with anything like comparable clarity.

That needs to change. It is not unreasonable for Palestinian opinion to resist peace proposals that do not clearly outline a viable path to personal security, dignity, and peace for members of the Palestinian people. Talk of resettlement on the West Bank and of development aid from rich countries is all very well, but ordinary Palestinians have every right to doubt that such talk will ever lead to real, effective help. Once war is over and peace reigns, many Western countries may forget their promises to aid the new Palestinian state. Even if they don't, the experience of foreign aid around the world does not suggest that ordinary citizens will reap great benefits from state to state transfers. The United States has sent Egypt many billions of dollars in foreign aid, but poverty in Egypt is still very high.

For many Palestinians there is another factor to consider: the future of the aid they now receive as refugees. Presumably once there is a peace treaty and the refugees all go "home" to Gaza and the West Bank, many donor nations will think the time has come to stop funneling hundreds of millions of dollars in refugee assistance. Some of this would no doubt be turned into foreign aid and disappear in the morass of corruption and incompetence that has already demonstrated such promising growth in the nascent Palestinian bureaucracy. But once there are no more refugees it would certainly seem as if refugee aid should at some point come to an end.

No land, no money, no future: many Palestinians could be excused for thinking that that is what "peace" on current terms would provide.

Now that Barak went about as far as Israel can in offering a territorial compromise, the peace process needs to move toward describing and preparing a significantly better future for a Palestinian population that has already suffered three generations of displacement and poverty. Part of this will have to involve a much more serious and focused discussion about compensation than we have yet had.

UN resolutions have always proposed just compensation as an alternative for Palestinians who for various reasons will be unable to return to their original homes and property. It is time to begin to turn this from empty words to the real prospect that a peace treaty between Israel and Palestine would bring concrete, substantial justice and benefits to the overwhelming majority of the Palestinian population.

This will take a lot of money. Somewhere between $50 billion and $100 billion has been paid to survivors of the Holocaust and their heirs since 1945; thanks in part to inflation, it is unlikely that fair compensation to the Palestinians and associated other costs will be much cheaper. Additional money will have to be raised to help Arab and other poor countries that agree to accept Palestinian refugees as immigrants and citizens. In simple fairness it will also be necessary to pay compensation to the millions of Jews who escaped or were forced to flee from their homes in the Arab world as violence and anti-Jewish feeling mounted during the years of struggle.

The United States can and should take the lead in proposing an international commission to allow individual Palestinians (and displaced Israelis) to certify their claims for compensation, and in pledging and raising money for a fund that will pay claims once Israel and Palestine are at peace. This money should go to individuals, not to state organizations, mass charities, or other intermediaries. It is individual compensation that should be paid to individual claimants. Palestinians would not need to prove, nor Israelis concede, wrongdoing for claims to be certified.

The American contribution should be a substantial, conspicuous, and inspiring sum. We will not have to pay any money until and unless there is a real peace treaty, and if there is a treaty the price, however high, will be worth paying.

Our European allies are able and should be willing to take up a substantial portion of the burden. Japan is concerned to see peace established in the region and can also help. The Gulf states should rouse themselves to heights of generosity at the prospect of increasing their own security and bringing relief to the suffering of their fellow religionists and Arabs. Private corporations that wish to enhance their images in the Middle East might also find it convenient to highlight their concern for Palestinian rights. Israel should certainly make a substantial contribution; part of this will be the value of the housing and infrastructure that will be returned to the Palestinians when the Israelis leave the West Bank. Since displaced Jews as well as Arabs will receive fair compensation, and since certification of claims does not require Israel to acknowledge specific acts of wrongdoing, a majority of Israelis should be able to accept this component of a comprehensive peace package.

There are other steps that can be taken to improve the situation of Palestinian refugees and address the problems of an increasingly despairing, embittered, and unskilled population, both in the occupied territories and in neighboring countries. If the United States cannot solve the political issue between Israelis and Palestinians, we can find ways to help individual Palestinians and

Palestinian families build better, more stable lives. These people should not have to keep their lives on hold for generation after generation, powerless to change their conditions until the elusive goal of a final settlement to this whole complex dispute can be reached. And we can perhaps help more of them leave the festering, economically blighted camp system of the refugee gulags and build new lives in other parts of the Arab and non-Arab world.

None of this will end the Israeli-Palestinian dispute anytime soon, or make the United States the favorite country of Palestinian nationalists. Palestinian society has been deeply wounded—by dispossession, by generations of dependent existence in refugee camps, by violence, by occupation, by fanatical propaganda—and there can be no overnight solutions to this complex human tragedy. But these are some of the ways we can begin to move beyond the current impasse and, hopefully, create a climate that little by little will become more conducive to a true and lasting peace.

The United States is firmly committed to Israel's survival within secure and defensible frontiers; that does not mean that we are or should be indifferent to the suffering of Palestinians. It would be good for the United States, good for Israel, and good for the Palestinians for the United States to become the conspicuous leader in a serious effort to improve the lives of the Palestinian people. If we are serious about the future of the Middle East, this is a problem we must face.

The third and final element of the kind of containment strategy we could find ourselves adopting also has its roots in our Cold War strategies. It is a simple strategy to describe, but under certain conditions it could become a very costly and difficult—but very necessary—strategy to implement.

Just as we resisted the Soviet Union's efforts to spread communism, we must now resist every effort of Arabian

Fascism and related movements to establish political control over any states anywhere in the world. To the peaceful preaching of authentic Islam we have no objection and offer no opposition—and indeed our diplomatic influence and from time to time our military power are ready to support people exercising their religious rights in peace—but the establishment of fascist governments by force and fraud is something that we must resist around the world again, it is hoped with the help of friends and allies inside and outside the Muslim world.

Sometimes this can get ugly. Adolf Hitler was legitimately appointed chancellor of the Weimar Republic. The legislation that established his dictatorship was passed by the Reichstag. Nevertheless there are few people today who would seriously argue that the rest of the world had no right to deal with the Hitler regime until 1939 when it invaded Poland.

It is impossible to predict how the political struggle against Arabian Fascism will evolve in the Middle East and elsewhere, but the possibility that there will be political movements whose acquisition of state power will be something that the United States would be bound to oppose cannot be ruled out.

Governments cannot have links to terror movements; terror movements, unless they change their ways, cannot become governments.

ELEVEN

Reconstructing the American Project

Dealing with the menace of a tactically flexible, morally ruthless, fanatical, and heavily armed Arabian Fascism that is implacably opposed to everything we value in an age of mass terror will be a difficult challenge. It is, however, not the only problem we face in the coming years. The political and economic relationships that sustained the American system through the Cold War and greatly assisted us during that conflict are in a state of advanced decay. We have lost the ability and to some degree the will to hold out the ideal of a harmonic convergence of classes, peoples, and nations in a Fordist paradise, and neither millennial capitalism nor the new domestic emphasis on American exceptionalism that shapes American Revival ideology has so far found a sufficiently attractive ideal to put forth in its place.

This is a problem for American foreign policy, and it is one that needs to be addressed, but we should not turn from the overoptimism of the "end of history" era between 1989 and 2001 to an equally excessive pessimism now. American power in the world continues to rest on strong foundations.

If we run down the checklist of interests that defined the American project through much of the twentieth century, there are solid reasons to believe that they remain within our reach. Europe is not about to become a hostile, rival superpower—even though there are some Europeans who would like that to happen. Indeed, it is far more likely that "Old Europe," "New Europe," and the United States will find a common approach to the Middle East that reenergizes their partnership than that the Cold War allies will become competitors and rivals as we move forward.

In Asia, the balance of forces and interests among Asian nations continues to favor the kind of balance of power the United States has traditionally supported in that part of the world. Better still, as China becomes stronger and richer, it also seems to be developing a deeper appreciation of the value of participating in the kind of system the United States has tried to build. China's growing economic might and diplomatic sophistication enable it to achieve more of its objectives within the kind of international system the United States hopes to stabilize in Asia. And while the future remains deeply uncertain and crises over issues like Taiwan can erupt at any moment, thanks to both Clinton and Bush administration policies, China and the United States seem closer to a genuine meeting of the minds than ever before.

The challenge of grand terror and Arabian Fascism in the Middle East is a real one, both to the kind of order the United States needs to promote there and to the security of the international system of commerce, trade, and investment that is such a vital element of the American system worldwide. Nevertheless, it appears that the United States has the resources and the will to contain and ultimately to defeat our enemies and so to prevail in this contest. Indeed, Osama Bin Laden, for all his villainy, may ultimately have done a great service to American power by challenging the American people to reexamine old assumptions and to engage with the rest of the world in a deeper and more purposeful way in the post–Cold War world.

Nothing in international politics is ever secure, but overall American hard power seems reasonably adequate to the defense of American strategic interests around the world. Both sharp military power and sticky economic power continue to work well. The most significant weakness in hard power is probably the deficiencies in our intelligence. The recent record of American intelligence is not what it ought to be. From the decline of the Soviet Union through the shockingly misguided assessments of Saddam's WMD programs in 2003, the United States has been blindsided by a whole series of important developments. Many analysts have concluded that better performance and better cooperation between the CIA and the FBI could have prevented the attacks of September 11. This performance needs to improve.

However, if American hard power is in reasonably good shape, American soft power is clearly experiencing difficulties.

There is a paradox here. The shift to millennial capitalism has given American hard power—both military and economic—a major boost. Before the shift was well under way, Americans were worried, and rightly so, about the challenges from Europe and Japan. As the United States explored the possibilities of the new, more competitive and dynamic form of capitalism emerging in the 1980s, it turned out that our society's greater ease with the individualism and inequality brought about by the new system made it easier for us to accept the pain of transition, and, therefore, reap the rewards. It appears that these advantages are long lasting; even as most of the rest of the world is still struggling to accept the disruptions of the transition, the United States is well into the second and third stages of the economic transformation. Conceivably, though by no means certainly, the economic advantage we are gaining will be comparable to the kind of global lead we enjoyed at the start of the twentieth century, and that Britain had for most of the nineteenth.

Yet it increasingly appears that this socioeconomic transformation has undermined or at least posed new challenges for America's soft power. As our capitalist model continues to shift in ways that alienate both mass and elite constituencies around the world, and as our national sense of ourselves continues to stress the exceptional and unique rather than the universal elements in the national character, we are scrambling to adjust to the consequences of these changes for both the sweet and the hegemonic dimensions of our soft power.

This is not, one should emphasize, just an "old European" or a Middle Eastern problem with American leadership. In Latin America, in South, Southeast, and East Asia, and in much of Africa including democratic South Africa, the United States and its international system are much less popular today than they were when the Berlin Wall fell. It is tempting, and not entirely implausible, to blame the Bush administration's controversial policies (above all the invasion of Iraq) and its sometimes brusque, confused, and ham-handed diplomacy for these problems, but in virtually every case the issues now troubling us were building up in the Clinton years. Long before George W. Bush started talking about the axis of evil, the unpopularity of the Clinton administration's response to the Asian financial crisis of 1997 alienated public opinion across the Far East, and the failure of the economic reforms supported both by the first President Bush and by President Clinton in Latin America had similarly dented support for U.S.-oriented policies in Brazil and Argentina. The failure of NAFTA to raise incomes in Mexico and the devastating effect it has had on peasant agriculture were failures of American policy in the 1990s. The wellspring of anti-Americanism that German Chancellor Gerhard Schroeder tapped in his reelection campaign in 2002 was no sudden mushroom springing up overnight out of nowhere. The economic straits that made his government so unpopular and forced his hand were in part the results of Germany's unwillingness and inability to adapt to the new economic conditions emanating from the United States.

We should not minimize the impact of Bush administration policies and rhetoric on global support for the United States. A series of international opinion polls shows widespread decline in support for and identification with the United States after September 11, 2001. But the erosion of American soft power had already begun when the World Trade Center was attacked. The Bush administration drove too heavy a vehicle out onto the frozen lake, but the ice was already melting. As we consider how to repair our grand strategy and the synthesis of hard and soft power that once worked so well for us, there are many who think that if we can just reverse and undo the changes of the Bush years we can get back to the calmer and more peaceful atmosphere of the "post-historical" nineties. This, I fear, is pure wishful thinking. The realities of American politics, accentuated by the public reaction to September 11 and the changes in the global economy already under way when President Clinton took the oath of office, are the fundamental drivers of instability and change in our system, not the errors and missteps of the Bush years.

While I agree with those who believe that a more focused and consistent effort to build diplomatic support abroad for American policy in the war on terror would reduce international tensions, I have already explained why I think that an awakened Jacksonian public opinion in the United States will force administrations of both parties toward a more aggressive set of responses than many of our allies want. The politically realistic alternative to a vigorous but sometimes messy and unilateral prosecution of the war on terror is not a purified, disciplined, and more multilateral engagement with the world on something like Europe's terms. For better or worse, American public opinion will not provide either the financial resources or the political support required by the measured, finely calibrated, and tightly reined foreign policy that a liberal and technocratic elite would like to carry out.

The dream of turning back the clock in economic policy is similarly unrealistic. Those who for both domestic and international reasons would like to see the United States return to a Fordist political economy and the harmonic convergence that went with it can dream, but they cannot shape policy. Nostalgic Fordists would like to bring back the welfare state, closed national markets, heavily regulated financial markets, and a greater state role in economic planning and policy. This seems to me to be as unfeasible as it is undesirable. The third quarter of the twentieth century was admirable in many ways, but I cannot believe that it represents the acme of human potential. Also, the world is not rich enough and poverty rare enough for the human race to turn its back on economic methods that, whatever their complications and consequences, hold out the promise of greatly enhanced living standards over time.

More than that, I do not believe that the genie of millennial capitalism can be forced back into the Fordist bottle. The quest for greater efficiency, productivity, and dynamism is not a feature of capitalism that can be dispensed with; it is the essence of capitalism, not an excrescence, and come what may it will find ways to fulfill itself. That quest corresponds to the desire implanted in every human individual and perhaps in every living thing to live, to grow, to explore, to search for light, and to fulfill the nature and hidden purpose within. I do not think we can stop this search for the light, and I would not stop it if I could.

The American task in coming years, I think, will be a different one: to build a new version of the old American system that is not only compatible with millennial political economy, but also derives new vigor and strength from it. Millennial capitalism has enormous potential to meet human needs and improve human lives. Already it has brought the industrial and technological revolutions to more people in the last two decades than the first industrial revolution reached in its first century.

Making the adjustment to an effective international system that functions well and enjoys widespread world support involves economic policy, but it also involves political, social, and cultural policy as well. Almost certainly there will be some changes in the way American power works and is perceived in the new international system. Millennial capitalism is a much more decentralized form of social organization than is Fordism. The mass society of mid-century America has become increasingly atomized and populist; elites are less and less able to influence what most Americans read, see, or think. As the millennial revolution moves out into the world, the same thing happens. Elites within states are less and less able to control the political process, and at the same time any given state, even a superpower, is less and less able to influence or control the foreign policy of other countries.

Whether in long-established and mature democracies like Germany or in younger ones like Mexico and South Korea, the grassroots activism, antiauthoritarianism, and decentralization that accompany the shift from Fordism to millennialism make it harder for the authorities in those countries to govern. It especially makes it harder for those governments to take unpopular stands in foreign policy. Increasingly people are no longer willing to passively accept their leaders' ideas of what is best. Most of the German foreign policy establishment hated the break with the United States over Iraq and wanted desperately to avoid the kind of quarrel with Washington that eventually took place. But the new, more populist atmosphere of German politics made this impossible. Germans, and many other publics around the world, are becoming more American in this sense, but that does not make the life of American foreign-policy makers any easier.

One of the chief signs of the new economy and political order in the world is that angels everywhere are being thrown out of their whirlwinds. Just as nobody is really in charge of where the United States goes or what it does, there are more and more countries where popular forces, business interests, and other elements of society have spun beyond the control of traditional elites and decision makers. V. S. Naipaul wrote of the changes in an earlier India as "a million mutinies"; soon, it will be up to a billion.

In this kind of atmosphere and against these kinds of forces, the United States cannot long preserve its global leadership if our image of primacy is that we are the angel directing the whirlwind of the world. While keeping our eye on our core national interests we are going to have to reinvent some of the ways we think about power and influence and we are certainly going to have to repackage our leadership for a world that we ourselves are working to make increasingly antiauthoritarian and suspicious of elites. Part of the culture clash between the administration of George W. Bush and the rest of the world was that the administration presented an old-fashioned vision of leadership to a world that is looking for a new approach.

Part of our response to these developments must be a new and more creative approach to issues of global governance. Currently the debate over institutions is stuck in a particularly sterile and unfavorable impasse. To be accepted worldwide, American power must be exerted at least to some extent within and in support of institutions and policies that enjoy support and legitimacy outside the United States. At the same time, the American political process consistently refuses to embrace the kinds of constraints and trade-offs that a fuller institutionalization of American power would require.

We have seen that there is no perfect solution to the tensions and contradictions surrounding the institutionalization of American power. But there is at least one promising avenue that could help reduce what is currently an unacceptable level of discontent with the world's institutional architecture in both the United States and much of the rest of the world.

The key institutions in the world were designed for a very different world than the one we inhabit today. Most of the global institutions were established in the aftermath of World War II. Most of Asia and Africa were still under imperial rule in those days; there were only about one fourth the number of independent states in 1945 as there are today.

The differences go much deeper. The world has become a much more diverse place than it used to be. Fifty years ago people could lump Asia, Africa, and Latin America together and talk about "underdeveloped countries." That term makes much less sense today. Brazil, Nigeria, India, China, and Iran have not grown together since 1945; they have followed very different paths. Africa, Asia, and Latin America are much more complicated than they used to be, and they are much less like one another.

The emergence of these differences, and the greater demand of peoples throughout the world to be heard on matters that affect them, is opening up a new kind of problem in international politics. The problem may be insoluble, but it cannot be ignored.

The problem is one of representation. On the one hand, only truly global institutions represent everybody. On the other hand, if everybody is equally and fairly represented, nobody has any real power. There are something like seven billion people in the world today. If each of us has an equal seven-billionth share in the decisions that affect us, then essentially none of us has any real ability to shape these decisions.

This is also a problem for mass democracies, of course. If every inhabitant of the United States had an equal share in political decisions, we would all have a three-hundred-millionth share. In mass democracies, this problem is addressed in two ways. State and local governments put as much power as possible into smaller units in which individual voters have more say. Your voice may be drowned out in the national conversation, but an energetic individual citizen can make his or her voice heard in a local school board election. Additionally, most citizens in mass democracies have party, regional, or other cultural and social affiliations which are large enough to have some representation at the national level. An individual woman who cares about feminist issues may not have much power over the way the United States works, but she can see that people who share her views do participate in policy making and have some influence on it. A gun owner can rejoice in the power of the NRA. Moreover, there is enough cultural similarity among the citizens of a mass democracy that most of the things that its government does are reasonably satisfactory to most of its citizens.

Global institutions cannot easily give individuals, affinity groups, and cultures the same sense of participation and empowerment. To the extent that such institutions include non-democratic states, the power of democracy is dramatically weakened when power moves from democratic states to mixed institutions. But even when this problem is not present—for example, in the European Union—international institutions are inevitably seen by many people as less legitimate and less accountable than national or local institutions would be.

The universal institutions of the 1940s still have a vital role to play. There are some things that only the United Nations can do. But there are also more and more things that the United Nations cannot do well.

Particularly under the Bush administration, the United States has spent more time and energy resenting the inadequacies of the current international architecture than in leading the way to its renewal. This is an opportunity lost. We need to become much more proactive when it comes to questions of global governance. To the degree that international institutions can be streamlined, improved, and reformed, the trade-offs that the United States faces will become less stark. If institutions work better (for others as well as for ourselves) it will be easier to work within them.

In general, we should be working on two major strategies. First, we should be moving much more creatively and purposefully than we now are to promote the restructuring and reform of the United Nations. Second, we should be seeking to supplement the United Nations with dynamic and flexible single-purpose and regional institutions.

Reform of the Security Council should be a top priority for the United States. Ideally, the number of European states that are permanent members should be reduced to reflect the changing global distribution of economic and military power, but it is unlikely that either Britain or France would ever agree to give up their seats to the European Union. In fact, Germany wants a permanent seat on the Security Council, and there are good arguments to support its candidacy.

Given these realities, the United States should support an expansion of the permanent membership of the Security Council to reflect the realities of today's world. Japan and India should obviously be permanent members. So should Brazil. There should be at least one African permanent member, and at least one member from the Muslim world. If Germany joins the Council, three additional non-European states should also receive permanent seats; no more than a third of the permanent members should be European.

Ideally, the United States should support the candidacies of Mexico, Brazil, Egypt, Nigeria, South Africa, India, Germany, Indonesia, and Japan to permanent, veto-wielding seats on the Security Council. There would be a slight reduction in the number of temporary seats on the Council to limit the increase in the total number of Security Council members. This would give Asia and Europe four permanent seats each, Africa three, Latin America two, and English-speaking North America one seat. The global south would have a clear majority of the permanent seats, but the interests of the industrial northern states would still be protected by their vetoes. In addition to the fourteen permanent members, there would be seven temporary members for a total membership of twenty-one.

It would be harder to get a consensus with fourteen veto-wielding members, but when a consensus was achieved, it would be seen as a much more legitimate and binding expression of the global political will than anything the Security Council can now produce.

Meanwhile, the United States should work to promote the development of regional institutions. If unwieldy universal institutions like the UN can play only somewhat more limited roles in the world than we once hoped, regional institutions can take up much of the slack. NATO and the European Union show that regional institutions can play a vital role in the peaceful evolution of regional security and prosperity. Mercosur in South America, ASEAN in Southeast Asia, and the African Union have similar ambitions that we can and should support at least in part.

In many cases regional institutions work better both for the United States and for the countries directly involved. American public opinion is suspicious of institutions that look like or aspire to be the building blocks of world government. Properly conceived, regional institutions will not trigger these concerns, and the United States will be able to work constructively with them under conservative and American Revival administrations as well as under liberal ones.

From the standpoint of other countries, the regional institutions give them a greater voice than universal institutions like the United Nations. Regional institutions can reflect the priorities and the cultural values of their members better than universal ones.

The development of regional institutions that promote collective security, economic integration, and other values may, as has happened with the European Union, create voices that can make themselves heard on the global scene, and give other countries more bargaining power vis-à-vis the United States. That will sometimes be inconvenient for the United States, but if at the same time these institutions stabilize security and economic issues in strategic parts of the world and provide barriers to would-be dominating regional hegemons, they will simultaneously promote important American national interests.

There is one more component of a strategy to renew and restore American soft power. The closest I have come yet to an understanding of the challenges ahead came in August 2001 when I spent a few days visiting the informal settlements and slums outside Cape Town, South Africa. The sadness and squalor of these settlements have been shocking visitors and locals for many years. In some ways, conditions got better with the end of apartheid as the new government improved the delivery of clean water, installed power lines, and provided assistance to families and cooperatives seeking to replace shacks made of everything from plywood to plastic garbage bags with more durable housing. On the other hand, crime is up and security is down since the end of apartheid, and, worse still, the people of these neighborhoods are falling victim in growing numbers to the HIV/AIDS pandemic.

As I walked through the alleys and streets of these neighborhoods I discovered some interesting facts. One was that the old (Fordist) method of improving housing by government subsidies and public housing was never going to work. Too many people needed houses and the government did not have enough money. That was going to be true even if Western governments substantially increased their development aid to South Africa: the human needs simply dwarf the resources available, and South Africa is by far the richest economy in sub-Saharan Africa. One can go to Zimbabwe, Nigeria, and dozens of other countries and see slums more desperate and people more deprived than anything in the Cape Flats.

But as I talked to the people of Khayelitsa—the settlement I spent the most time in—I learned something more hopeful. At 2001 prices, a modest but adequate three-bedroom house on its own lot, connected to sewer, water, and electricity lines, costs about $3,200. Houses of this type are much larger and more desirable than the $2,300 homes supplied by the largest government program in the region. If the people in Khayelitsa could buy houses the way Americans do, making a 10 percent down payment on a thirty-year loan, most families would qualify for mortgages. Many families pay rents on shacks that are double the mortgage payments they would need to buy a real home.

No banks in South Africa make $3,200 mortgage loans. In Khayelitsa it is hard to find an ATM, much less a bank branch, and if there are any realtors or mortgage brokers in the community, I didn't see them or meet anyone who had.

There are other things missing in Khayelitsa. You will see chickens and pigs slaughtered by the side of the road for sale to people coming home from work. You will see vendors with small piles of fruit and clothing. You will see people washing clothes at communal taps. But you will not see neighborhood stores and commercial districts in most of the settlements. The reason, once again, has less to do with poverty than with lack of access to finance. Small-business bank loans are simply not available for the entrepreneurs of Khayelitsa.

When I look at these scenes, and I have seen similar

ones throughout the developing world, I despair if I think in Fordist terms.

But millennial capitalism might be different. It has taken financial engineering to new heights. Information technology has drastically reduced transaction costs. Millennial capitalism has created vast, deep, and flexible international capital markets that could, in theory, channel first world capital to banks and other institutions that would make mortgage loans to the people of Khayelitsa and the thousands of similar settlements around the world.

Fordism saw the creation of mass mortgage and financial service markets in the advanced industrial democracies. Can millennial capitalism internationalize this phenomenon so that one day German pension funds and Japanese institutional investors can add Brazilian and South African mortgage-backed securities to their portfolios?

When I think about the future of American soft power, I think about global finance turned to meeting human needs, and about Khayelitsa, and Rozina in Rio de Janeiro, and Ebute Metta outside Lagos.

Closer to home, we need to do more to address the enormous problems of Mexico, Central America, and the Caribbean—places whose fates are increasingly intertwined with ours. For social, political, and economic reasons, the United States needs to find better ways to help these countries grow—and to help Cuba find a path toward a prosperous and free future when the long reign of Fidel Castro finally comes to an end.

The state of our region matters more to our domestic welfare and to our global position than most Americans have yet understood. As immigration from the region grows, and as both legal and illicit trade rapidly expands, Americans have begun to understand the increasingly important connections that unite the countries of the region—although so far our concern is motivated more by fear than by a hopeful vision of what a more prosperous region would mean for the United States.

But there is more. Our immediate neighborhood should be an example to the world of how democratic governance, access to American markets, and cooperative economic and diplomatic relationships with the United States bring concrete benefits to poor countries willing to play the game. If the countries in our own immediate region have not prospered, what promise do our policies and proposals hold out for other countries, farther from our markets and from our concerns? If the United States is neither willing nor able to alleviate poverty on its own doorstep, what evidence can we offer the rest of the world that we are working to build a better future? The poor state of our region is a telling and deeply damaging criticism of America's role in the world. If we cannot help people in Mexico, Jamaica, Colombia, and the Dominican Republic live dramatically better lives, what does the *Pax Americana* offer poor people (that is, the overwhelming majority) in countries like Nigeria, Indonesia, India, and Brazil?

President Bush's initial instinct to make U.S.–Mexico relations a pivot of his foreign policy was correct, and so is the view, now widely shared among both Republicans and Democrats, that the way to help Mexico and the region is to engage in a process of regional economic integration.

Opening U.S. borders through free trade agreements was an early step toward using American prosperity and American markets to lift living standards in the region, but trade is not enough. NAFTA has been a brilliant success in increasing trade (since NAFTA went into effect in 1994 Mexico's exports to the United States have grown from $51 billion to $135 billion), but real, inflation-adjusted wages in Mexico have fallen 15 percent since 1994, and the gap between the impoverished south and the relatively prosperous north has grown.* As President Fox frequently points out, 51 percent of Mexicans—50 million people—live in poverty, and 17.9 million live in severe poverty (on less than $2 per day), including 7.1 million out of Mexico's 8.7 million indigenous people. Statistics in Central America and the Caribbean paint similar pictures. This cannot go on without creating serious domestic problems for the United States as immigration, crime, drug trafficking, and other social ills spread across our permeable borders.

In returning his attention to Mexico in early 2004, President Bush proposed revisiting the conditions of illegal workers in the American economy and developing ways to ease the path for Mexicans and others eager to work in the United States on a temporary basis, and who are willing to take on jobs Americans do not want. I support these initiatives, though more attention should be paid to the potential impact of these measures on low-income Americans and legal residents. Nevertheless, like NAFTA, limited guest worker programs will not give Mexico and Caribbean countries the development boost they need. There are limits to how many guest workers and immigrants the United States is willing and able to absorb.

There is a third option that would be much more popular in the United States than trade and guest worker agreements—and would ultimately have a more substantial impact on regional prosperity. In fact, by enlisting the help of the region in solving one of our major social problems, we can help our neighbors make the transition to first world prosperity much more rapidly than even most optimists dare to hope.

More than one hundred million U.S. citizens are projected to reach age sixty-five in the next thirty years.

* U.S. Department of Commerce, *U.S. International Trade in Goods and Services: Annual Revisions for 2002* (Washington, D.C.: Government Printing Office, April 2003), CB-03-94, BEA-03-21.

Many of these seniors will not be able to afford the type of retirement they expect—especially as the cost of retirement housing and other services skyrockets due to the rapidly increasing demand. At the same time, millions of workers from the region enter the United States, often illegally, to work in health care and other industries that serve the elderly.

Why should this migration be only one way? Why not allow—encourage—U.S. citizens to retire where costs are lower, and where their consumer spending can encourage local economic development?

The U.S. (and Canada) should negotiate agreements with interested and willing partners in the region to provide favorable tax, customs, and other treatment to encourage American (and Canadian) citizens to retire south of the border—and provide a suitable legal framework for issues like taxation, insurance, property rights, and inheritance. The president would also ask Congress to provide the necessary legislation that would allow qualified and licensed health care facilities to receive reimbursement under Medicare for treating eligible Americans. These reimbursements would be at some discounted percentage of the payments offered in the U.S., allowing the U.S. government to save money from the lower health costs in Mexico and elsewhere.

This kind of development policy is win-win. It is not foreign aid; it will not destroy American jobs. (Employment in health services will continue to grow rapidly as the U.S. population ages, even if a substantial number of Americans choose to spend some of their retirement abroad.) Taking advantage of Mexico's lower costs will reduce the Medicare deficits that pose an even greater threat to the long-term fiscal health of the U.S. Treasury than Social Security, while creating, literally, millions of new jobs and billions of dollars in new investments in the region. And by creating hundreds of thousands of jobs in Mexico and the Caribbean this policy reduces the pressure for illegal immigration. Studies estimate that every retired household pumps an estimated $55,000 per year into local economies. In addition to spending on consumables and medical care, there would be major investments in housing, infrastructure, recreational, and tourism facilities and a whole range of related activities. Florida was a swamp and Arizona was a desert before waves of retirees transformed those once sleepy economies. Hosting U.S. retirees is a way for countries like Mexico to create jobs, finance infrastructure development, and jump-start lasting economic growth.

This is millennial capitalism at work. It is not foreign aid; it is not an entitlement program. It does not force anybody to do anything. Americans who do not want to retire in Mexico or Costa Rica can retire in Ohio or Florida. Countries who do not want to participate in this program are free to stay out of it. But those who would like more choices can enjoy them.

A regional retirement initiative like this is also millennial in that it gives the poor better access to capitalism, rather than trying to shield them from it. It increases the opportunities for citizens of Mexico and neighboring countries to find new kinds of work and build new kinds of businesses to serve a new and prosperous market.

Like the development of mortgage markets for ordinary working people in developing countries, the promotion of regional retirement is a way to use the potential of new technologies to improve the lives of people in both rich and poor countries. When I think about the future of American power, I think about the enormous potential of millennial capitalism—its mobility of capital, its capacity to abolish distance, its ability to raise human productivity and to facilitate the rise of new industries and new markets—turned to the service of human need.

American foreign policy is not just the business of the American government. As we seek to build a sustainable global system in an era of millennial capitalism and accelerating globalization, the American people must take a direct hand in international affairs. American civil society must become more deeply engaged in addressing the world's most urgent problems. Poverty and HIV/AIDS in both South Asia and Africa are conditions that Fordist programs of bureaucratically administered foreign aid are largely powerless to address. American civil society can do much more than it is now doing. Perhaps the United States can be the first of the G-7 countries to reach the goal of providing 0.7 percent of GDP in development assistance. However, we would do this in our own, exceptionalistic, and post-Fordist way, including channels like private philanthropy and faith-based charity. It might even be that aid given in this way would ultimately have more success than aid spent in the old ways. Presidents can and should use the bully pulpit to encourage this deeper engagement, directly and by convening religious, philanthropic, and other leaders together. In the end, though, the energy and commitment of the American people will determine how successful this aspect of our foreign policy will be.

Despite the serious problems we face, and despite the enormous damage our soft power has sustained in recent years, I am optimistic about the future. Our current problems seem so acute in large part because the attacks of September 11 came at a particularly vulnerable moment in the history of the American system. By 2001 the transition from Fordism to millennial capitalism had entered a critical stage. The transition was causing enormous pain and discomfort to governments, powerful interest groups, and cultural leaders in both Europe and the developing world, but the benign features of millennial capitalism were still relatively underdeveloped.

This is going to change. To begin with, the very intelligent and creative entrepreneurs and civil servants of many of the world's economies are increasingly finding ways to promote the transition to millennial capitalism within their own societies. The United States may have been the first country to begin the shift, but it will not be the last. France has led the intellectual charge against the shift from Fordism, but France is also moving very rapidly to restructure and recast its economy to take full advantage of the opportunities the new system affords. As more and more companies and economic sectors make the shift in more and more countries around the world, millennial capitalism will be seen less and less as a specifically American mechanism and come to look more and more like a natural and even welcome form of progress. Just as Fordism took different shapes in the United States, western Europe, and other parts of the world, so, too, are we likely to see more forms of millennial capitalism taking shape.

As capitalism has gradually unfolded and developed through first Western and now world history, there have frequently been moments when cultural and social forces lagged behind the economic forces that were building new realities. The industrial revolution burst upon societies with no experience of mass urbanization. It took time for society to understand the trade cycle, the terrible vulnerabilities that industrial workers, cut off from the land, experienced in times of mass unemployment, and the many other new phenomena of industrial society. It took time for values and political and social institutions to adjust to the new realities, and in some countries the turbulence associated with these transitions led to such terrible historic derailments as the Bolshevik Revolution in Russia.

Today, once again we are confronting economic changes that are outstripping our ability to adjust and ameliorate them. The new forms of interdependence and association known as globalization are part of this phenomenon. So, too, are the effects of more dynamic competition within national economies.

The world is not quite ready for all the changes we are

experiencing. Just as in the early decades of the industrial revolution, it is more common to find movements of reactionary protest and hopelessly utopian longing than to find practical and realistic methods to use the new economic system to solve the problems that it causes.

There are promising signs that the world's social imagination is catching up with the new opportunities. The work of the Peruvian economist Hernando de Soto has laid out the importance of private property and access to credit for poverty alleviation. The microcredit movement, which, like de Soto, enjoys support from both "left wing" and "right wing" constituencies, is also building a body of knowledge and experience about how access to capitalism can improve the living conditions of the poor. The growing consensus, again, on both the right and the left, that giving women greater access to education and economic opportunity is a key to development also reflects the rise of a new philosophy of empowerment. The poor need access to capitalism more than they need protection from it.

I think the future of American foreign policy may lie in bridging the gap between the power of capital and the people of places like Khayelitsa. Enabling ordinary people around the world to change their lives by the power of capital can accomplish more than building houses, businesses, hospitals, mosques, churches, and schools. It can build a new version of the world system, one that depends less and less on American military power and more and more on the attachment of people around the world to a set of values and beliefs.

At the end of the day, the 5 percent minus of the world's population who live in the United States cannot impose a world order on the 95 percent plus of humanity beyond our frontiers. The United States must stand for values and freedoms that make sense not only to ourselves but to our partners and friends around the world.

Franklin Delano Roosevelt more than any other single person was the architect of American world power in the Fordist era. Under his leadership, the United States built the New Deal at home and laid the foundations for the world system that under his successors would bring more prosperity and more freedom to more people than at any time in the history of the world.

All through his life Roosevelt's deepest personal and political values bore the imprint of the charismatic and occasionally fearsome founding headmaster of the boarding school FDR attended in his youth. Endicott Peabody summed up his personal philosophy in a Latin phrase that became the motto of his school: *Cui Servire Est Regnare.* Often translated as "whose service is perfect freedom," the phrase carries the idea that one cannot rule without serving both God and the human race.

This idea runs through Roosevelt's lifework like a golden thread. Capitalism could save itself from the Depression only by meeting the needs of ordinary working people. The United States could rise to world power only by helping to solve the problems of the world.

The key to American foreign policy (and domestic policy, too, for that matter) today is that we must hold fast to Franklin Roosevelt's values even as we discard most of his methods.

As someone greater even than Roosevelt put it, "Whoever wishes to be first among you must become the servant of all." This is not just a piece of feel-good religious advice. It is a sober statement about the way enduring power works. It is the task to which the American people and our friends and allies around the world have been called, and much depends on how well we fulfill it.

ACKNOWLEDGMENTS

A book like this may list only one author on its
cover, but in our society the writing of books is a
complicated social endeavor that involves the
cooperation and support of many people. The idea for
Power, Terror, Peace, and War came to me in the summer of 2003; without the enthusiasm of my longtime lit-
erary agent and dear friend Geri Thoma the idea would
have died right away. Richard Haass, then just stepping
into his new responsibilities at the Council on Foreign
Relations, allowed me to set my other obligations and
deadlines to the side to dedicate all my time to this book.
Jonathan Segal, my longtime editor at Knopf, assisted by
Ida Giragossian, provided just the right mix of encourage-
ment and pressure so that I was able to deliver the manuscript on time.

As always, my writing process relies heavily on the
advice and comments of close friends and colleagues. The
personal, professional, and intellectual debts I owe to Les
Gelb can never be repaid—and I hope to fall deeper and
deeper in his debt as the years go by. Jim Lindsay, who
joined the Council this summer as director of studies, gave
the manuscript a thorough, searching, and extremely helpful reading. Julia Sweig, Henry Siegman, and Rachel Bron-
son made helpful suggestions.

This book benefited from study groups in Los Angeles

and New York. I'm grateful to Robert Abernathy for his gracious hospitality and for his generosity in underwriting the expenses of the Los Angeles group. James Chace, who has provided me with friendship and guidance at many critical points in my career, chaired the New York study group with his usual grace and flair.

I particularly want to thank the junior staff of the Council on Foreign Relations in Washington and New York who organized and led study group sessions on the manuscript. Chris Angell and Ian Cornwall presided in New York and Michael McCarthy and Kathleen Jennings in Washington. Junior staff study groups continue to be among the most useful reviews that my manuscripts receive.

The Council on Foreign Relations is an extraordinary organization; I never fail to be amazed and touched by the dedication of my friends and colleagues to the Council and its mission. Since the attacks of September 11, the women and men of this staff have redoubled their effort to contribute to the understanding of American foreign policy and the challenges we face. Building on Les Gelb's foundation, Richard Haass has continued to make the Council a more dynamic and important part of the American foreign policy debate. Mike Peters and Jan Murray have worked miracles to make the Council a place where scholars and thinkers have the support needed to do their jobs.

Charlie Day and his colleagues Albert Andrade, Alice McLoughlin, Ginny Parrott, Chris Sierra, Deepak Trivedi, and Richard Wawzycki in the Information Services department have rescued lost documents, replaced malfunctioning equipment, and generally managed my incompetence with machinery of all kinds with grace and skill. Santo Ine Alers, Frank Alverez, Angel Cordova, Gilbert Falcon, Phil Falcon, Ian Noray, Anthony Ramirez, Edwin Santiago, Derek Velez, and Lawrence White routinely go far beyond the call of duty and have made my office at the Council the most welcoming and efficient workspace I have ever had. Alicia Siebenaler, Jean-Michel Oriol, and Avery Alpha staff the Studies Department; without them the Department and Fellows would grind to a halt. Jan Hughes, Donna Sardella, and Kerryn Kletter, who run Human Resources at the Council, have consistently helped me find and recruit extraordinary research associates. The reference librarians, Lilita Gusts, Michelle McKowen, Barbara Miller, Ming Er Qiu, Christine Quinn, Marcia Sprules, and Connie Stagnaro, as always, can reach the unreachable source and find the unfindable fact. David Kellogg, Lisa Shields, Irina Faskianos, Elise Lewis, Jeff Reinke, Jacqui Schien, Bernard M. Gwertzman, Patricia Dorff, Marie Strauss, Abigail Zoba, and Jennifer Manuel have been more than generous with their time and counsel.

I owe a special debt to Bryan Gunderson, the research associate who worked closely with me throughout the writing of this book. Bryan had a real baptism by fire at the Council; he joined us just as I plunged into the writing and had to learn his way around this very complex institution at a time when life was even more hectic than usual. Without his tireless and good-natured help, I could never have finished this manuscript, or seen it through editing and revision, on such a tight schedule. I am also grateful to Charles Edel, who joined our group while the manuscript was in editing and made substantial contributions to the finished product. I am extremely grateful to Luis Lugo and the Pew Forum on Religion and Public Life whose support enabled Charles to join the Council.

Finally, I would like to thank a group of members of the Council on Foreign Relations who have supported my work financially and through their counsel over a period of several years. I am especially grateful to Henry Arnhold, Kimball Chen, Robert Chaves, Mark Fisch, John Guth, Tom and Janine Hill, and Frank Hoch. The interest, support, and generosity of the members is what enables the Council on Foreign Relations to maintain its standards of quality and independence; I am honored that so many of them have seen fit to interest themselves in my work.

A NOTE ABOUT THE AUTHOR

Walter Russell Mead is the Henry A. Kissinger Senior Fellow for United States Foreign Policy at the Council on Foreign Relations. He is the author of *Mortal Splendor: The American Empire in Transition* and *Special Providence: American Foreign Policy and How It Changed The World*, 2002 winner of the Lionel Gelber Award for the best book in English on international relations, and winner in 2003 of the *Premio Acqui Storia* for the most important historical work published in Italian. Mr. Mead is a contributing editor at the *Los Angeles Times* and has had a distinguished career in journalism. In 1997 he was a finalist for a National Magazine Award in the category of essays and criticism; in 1992 he won an Olive Tree Award for work that appeared in *Harper's* magazine. His work frequently appears in leading newspapers, magazines and foreign policy journals in the United States and abroad. A native of South Carolina, he lives in Jackson Heights, New York.

A NOTE ON THE TYPE

The text of this book was composed in Trump Mediæval. Designed by Professor Georg Trump (1896–1985) in the mid-1950s, Trump Mediæval was cut and cast by the C. E. Weber Type Foundry of Stuttgart, Germany. The roman letter forms are based on classical prototypes, but Professor Trump has imbued them with his own unmistakable style. The italic letter forms, unlike those of so many other typefaces, are closely related to their roman counterparts. The result is a truly contemporary type, notable for both its legibility and its versatility.

COMPOSED BY
Creative Graphics,
Allentown, Pennsylvania

PRINTED AND BOUND BY
R. R. Donnelley & Sons,
Harrisonburg, Virginia

DESIGNED BY
Iris Weinstein